D1318074

Jamie Foxx

by Terri Dougherty

LUCENT BOOKS

An imprint of Thomson Gale, a part of The Thomson Corporation

THOMSON

TM

GALE

Detroit • New York • San Francisco • San Diego • New Haven, Conn.
Waterville, Maine • London • Munich

On cover: Jamie Foxx rehearses for the 2005 MTV Video Music Awards in Miami, Florida.

© 2006 Thomson Gale, a part of The Thomson Corporation.

Thomson and Star Logo are trademarks and Gale and Lucent Books are registered trademarks used herein under license.

For more information, contact
Lucent Books
27500 Drake Rd.
Farmington Hills, MI 48331-3535
Or you can visit our Internet site at http://www.gale.com

ALL RIGHTS RESERVED.
No part of this work covered by the copyright hereon may be reproduced or used in any form or by any means—graphic, electronic, or mechanical, including photocopying, recording, taping, Web distribution or information storage retrieval systems—without the written permission of the publisher.

Every effort has been made to trace the owners of copyrighted material.

LIBRARY OF CONGRESS CATALOGING-IN-PUBLICATION DATA

Dougherty, Terri.
    Jamie Foxx / by Terri Dougherty.
        p. cm. — (People in the news)
    Includes bibliographical references and index.
    Summary: Discusses the life and career of comedian, actor, and musician Jamie Foxx, who won the 2005 Best Actor Academy Award for his portrayal of Ray Charles in the film Ray.
    ISBN 1-59018-848-9 (hard cover : alk. paper) 1. Foxx, Jamie. 2. Actors—United States—Biography. I. Title. II. Series.
    PN2287.F632D68 2006
    792.02'8092—dc22

                                                                                2005028854

Printed in the United States of America

Contents

Fame and celebrity are alluring. People are drawn to those who walk in fame's spotlight, whether they are known for great accomplishments or for notorious deeds. The lives of the famous pique public interest and attract attention, perhaps because their experiences seem in some ways so different from, yet in other ways so similar to, our own.

Newspapers, magazines, and television regularly capitalize on this fascination with celebrity by running profiles of famous people. For example, television programs such as *Entertainment Tonight* devote all of their programming to stories about entertainment and entertainers. Magazines such as *People* fill their pages with stories of the private lives of famous people. Even newspapers, newsmagazines, and television news frequently delve into the lives of well-known personalities. Despite the number of articles and programs, few provide more than a superficial glimpse at their subjects.

Lucent's People in the News series offers young readers a deeper look into the lives of today's newsmakers, the influences that have shaped them, and the impact they have had in their fields of endeavor and on other people's lives. The subjects of the series hail from many disciplines and walks of life. They include authors, musicians, athletes, political leaders, entertainers, entrepreneurs, and others who have made a mark on modern life and who, in many cases, will continue to do so for years to come.

These biographies are more than factual chronicles. Each book emphasizes the contributions, accomplishments, or deeds that have brought fame or notoriety to the individual and shows how that person has influenced modern life. Authors portray their subjects in a realistic, unsentimental light. For example, Bill Gates—the cofounder and chief executive officer of the software giant Microsoft—has been instrumental in making personal computers the most vital tool of the modern age. Few dispute his business savvy, his perseverance, or his technical expertise, yet critics say he is ruthless in his dealings with competitors and driven more by his desire to maintain Microsoft's dominance in the computer industry than by an interest in furthering technology.

In these books, young readers will encounter inspiring stories about real people who achieved success despite enormous obstacles. Oprah Winfrey—the most powerful, most watched, and wealthiest woman on television today—spent the first six years of her life in the care of her grandparents while her unwed mother sought work and a better life elsewhere. Her adolescence was colored by promiscuity, pregnancy at age fourteen, rape, and sexual abuse.

Each author documents and supports his or her work with an array of primary and secondary source quotations taken from diaries, letters, speeches, and interviews. All quotes are footnoted to show readers exactly how and where biographers derive their information and provide guidance for further research. The quotations enliven the text by giving readers eyewitness views of the life and accomplishments of each person covered in the People in the News series.

In addition, each book in the series includes photographs, annotated bibliographies, timelines, and comprehensive indexes. For both the casual reader and the student researcher, the People in the News series offers insight into the lives of today's newsmakers—people who shape the way we live, work, and play in the modern age.

Putting Many Talents to Work

As an actor, comedian, and musician, the multitalented Jamie Foxx has made his mark on the entertainment world in a number of ways. His most prestigious honor came in 2005, when he won an Oscar for his performance as singer Ray Charles in the movie *Ray*. He is also a talented musician and comedian, and he used those talents as stepping-stones to an acclaimed acting career.

Foxx's interest in music and comedy began in childhood. He attended college on a music scholarship and used his talent as a pianist to move out of the small town in Texas where he grew up. He wanted to be a singer, but a stand-up comedy stint changed his mind. Having also shown a knack for doing impersonations from the time he was a child, he turned his career aspirations from music to comedy after being rewarded with applause on the stand-up stage. Foxx then used the success he achieved as a stand-up performer to make his way into television and movie comedies.

Foxx's many skills have helped his career move steadily along. After his first television show ended, Foxx made a CD called *Peep This*. When the movie roles he wanted did not come his way, he went back to television. When one avenue comes to a dead end, he always has another to turn to, and his career strategy has been to do whatever he could in order to continue working. Early in his career this led to parts in some questionable movies, such as *Booty Call* and *Breakin' All the Rules,* but Foxx's goal has always been to keep his name in the mix, even if it meant taking some forgettable roles.

Jamie Foxx entertains fans at the MTV Video Music Awards in 2005.

Perseverance has been another hallmark of Foxx's life and career. As a child Foxx took piano lessons, developing the discipline necessary to learn to play well. In his professional life, he has rebounded after disappointing auditions (he lost out on a role in *Jerry Maguire*) and performances (a reviewer for *Held Up* said he lacked the talent to carry a film) to earn acclaim for his roles in *Any Given Sunday, Ali,* and *Ray.* The title role in *Ray* became his only after he proved to Ray Charles that he had the determination needed to master a difficult piano piece. Foxx's perseverance during the audition earned him the role that would take his career to a new level.

Foxx's many talents for impersonation, music, and drama merged in his role in *Ray.* The result was a potent performance, and the Oscar win it brought gave Foxx the clout he needed to have more input into the movies and music he makes. Foxx now has the influence to make films with Eddie Murphy and Colin Farrell and to perform music with Kanye West and Twista. After he won the Oscar, one of his first moves was to make a CD. It was titled *Unpredictable,* a fitting name for a recording from a man whose career can take him in a variety of directions.

Chapter 1

From Texas to L.A.

The foundation for Jamie Foxx's success was laid during his childhood. From an early age he showed promise as an athlete and musician. Foxx was raised by his grandparents, and they made sure he did not waste his skills. Foxx's family was not wealthy, but his grandparents helped him develop the character he would need to make the most of his talent.

Eric Bishop

Jamie Foxx was born in Terrell, Texas, on December 13, 1967. However, his name was not Jamie Foxx when he was born. His parents gave their son the name Eric Morlon Bishop, and that was the name he was known by when he was growing up in Terrell. He changed his name to Jamie Foxx after he moved to California and began performing.

Jamie's parents were Louise Annette Talley and Shaheed Abdullah. His mother was a homemaker and his father was a stockbroker, and they separated when Foxx was seven months old. His parents felt they could not accept the responsibility of raising a child, so Foxx was adopted by his grandparents, Mark and Estelle Talley. They had also adopted his mother thirteen years earlier, and they would now raise her son.

Foxx grew up with his grandparents in Terrell. The town of 14,000 people is about 30 miles (48 km) east of Dallas and is part of the Dallas metropolitan area. Foxx and his grandparents lived in a poorer section of town, but although his grandparents did not have a great deal of money Foxx did not feel that he was deprived of anything during his childhood. To him, being raised by grandparents who loved him, and living in a community where he felt secure, was enough. "Though we were broke, I had a great childhood," he said. "No killing, none of that. Just good fun. It wasn't a 'hood back then. It was a neighborhood."[1]

Foxx's grandfather worked as a yardman, and his grandmother worked as a maid and also operated a nursery for young children. Estelle Talley was fifty-seven years old when Foxx was adopted. As an adult, Foxx recalled his grandmother being a strict, but loving, disciplinarian. He sometimes felt his grandmother did not understand him because of the distance between their ages. "There was a generation gap," he said. "She didn't understand me, but she raised me with an iron fist."[2]

*Foxx displays an issue of his Texas hometown's newspaper, the **Terrell Tribune**, which features an article about his Golden Globe nominations.*

Absent Parents

Under his grandmother's watchful eye, Foxx grew up to be a polite, well-behaved child. When he was in grade school, his teachers and classmates spoke well of him. His respectful attitude was reinforced by his family's Christian beliefs. His grandmother was a churchgoing woman who often took her grandson with her when she attended services.

While Foxx was growing up with caring grandparents, he had little contact with his birth parents. They lived in Dallas but did not visit him and never gave him a reason for remaining distant. Although he would have liked to have known his mother and father better, they were not part of his life as he grew up. Foxx later said that while he was a child, his mother "was doing her thing. She was young, pretty, living in Dallas."[3]

Foxx's mother and father divorced when he was six years old. His mother later married a man named George Dixon and had two daughters, Deidra and Diondra. Foxx would eventually become close to his stepfather and sisters, but would always have a distant relationship with his mother.

Inner Strength

Foxx's grandmother had an unwavering faith in her grandson that helped him overcome the hurt of being unwanted by his parents. From the time he was very young, Estelle Talley noticed that Foxx had talent and was determined to encourage him to use it to make something of himself. The nursery school she ran had a library of books for children, and when she saw Foxx reading at a young age she realized that he was a bright child. Because Estelle Talley felt that her grandson was capable of one day accomplishing great things, she would not let failure be an option for him.

Although their family was poor, Foxx's grandmother did not want him to grow up with the attitude that he was less important or less worthy than people who had more money. She insisted that he carry himself with dignity and wanted her grandson to be self-assured and well mannered. "She told me to stand up straight," he said years later. "Put your shoulders back. Act like you got some sense."[4]

Foxx's grandmother also wanted him to be proud and independent. She discouraged him from eating meals at neighbors' homes, in case his large appetite would make their neighbors think that his family did not have enough food of their own. When they were out in public, she expected him to act properly. If he did not, there were consequences. "We would go places. And I would wild out. And she would say, 'Act like you've been somewhere,'" he says. "And then when I would act the fool, she would beat me. She would whup me. And she could get an Oscar for the way she whupped me because she was great at it."[5]

After the painful discipline came the explanation, as Foxx's grandmother would take time to explain to her grandson why she went to such extremes to keep him well behaved. She was hard on him because she wanted him to act like a Southern gentleman. Foxx eventually understood why his grandmother insisted that he act properly and show respect toward others.

Young Performer

In addition to being adamant that her grandson act properly, Foxx's grandmother also insisted he take music lessons. Although his grandmother's Christian beliefs kept the family from listening to pop music in their house, Foxx was allowed to practice the piano. Foxx learned to play the piano when he was three years old, and his piano lessons took precedence over any other interests or activities. When he grew older and also became a talented football player, he had to leave the practice field when it was time for his piano lesson. His grandmother thought that Foxx was musically talented and if his ability was nurtured properly, it would offer him a chance at a prosperous future.

In addition to a talent for music, young Foxx also had the ability to make people laugh. This came so naturally to him that when he was seven years old he told his friends that he wanted to be a stand-up comedian one day. This was not his only goal. He was also aware of his musical talent, and he said he wanted to be a singer as well.

While Foxx's musical talent was evident through his piano-playing ability, his inclination toward comedy came out at school.

Jamie Foxx credits his grandmother with teaching him to be self-assured and well mannered.

By the time he was in second grade he could make his classmates break out in laughter. Foxx's teacher encouraged his talent by using it as a way to keep the class in line. When the class behaved, Foxx's teacher rewarded them by giving Foxx time to tell jokes.

Having played the piano since he was three years old, Foxx (left) was a top candidate to depict musician Ray Charles in the hit movie Ray.

A neighbor also influenced Foxx to take his talents seriously. Richard Tolbert lived across the street from Foxx, and although he was small in stature he was the quarterback of the Terrell High School football team. Foxx was impressed by Tolbert's winning attitude and saw how his heart for the game gave him the edge over larger players. Tolbert encouraged Foxx not to waste time just fooling around. "He asked me, 'Are you going to be corny all your life, or are you going to do something?'" Foxx later recalled. "That stuck out in my mind more than anything." [6]

Putting His Talent to Work

While comedy would eventually be Foxx's ticket to success, it did not get him his first paying job. As a talented piano player with a churchgoing grandmother, he found opportunities to play the piano at church during Sunday morning services. He also sang, and at age thirteen he became the choir leader and music director at New Hope Baptist Church. He earned $75 each Sunday, providing extra income for his cash-strapped family.

Foxx was happy to help his grandmother and grandfather by earning some money himself. He witnessed how his grandmother had to be immediately available to her employer, sometimes getting early morning telephone calls telling her to report to her job as a maid. Foxx disliked the way his grandmother was treated, and it made him determined to one day find success outside of Terrell.

Racial Divide

As a teen Foxx also earned money for his family by playing piano at wine-and-cheese parties for the area's wealthier citizens. However, he did not feel accepted by the white community. A

Making Music

As a teenager, Jamie Foxx set high standards for himself when it came to performing in front of people. For a time he and some high school friends had a rhythm and blues band called Leather and Lace. Years later he acknowledged that the group had sounded terrible.

The group's lowest point came during a performance in front of the whole school. To his dismay, Foxx found that the drum machine had been unplugged and the rhythm track was erased. Embarrassed, Foxx left the stage and went into the school hallway, where he could not hold back his tears. Foxx's friend Gilbert Willie recalled this reaction in the April 2005 article "Foxx-y 'Gentleman.'" "Jamie stormed off the stage and into the halls, and when we found him he had these irate tears coming from his eyes. He was so embarrassed. He had a passion for wanting everything to be correct."

racial divide that existed in Terrell also made Foxx dream of one day leaving his hometown.

Foxx had became acutely aware of the differences between black and white cultures at a young age. He heard derogatory racial slurs directed at blacks and learned that blacks were not welcome in some areas of town. When Foxx would travel to nearby communities as a member of the high school tennis team, children as young as third and fourth graders would call him names such as "porch monkey." He later recalled, "The opposite side of the tracks was drummed into you. When I'd go to the other side of the tracks, it was definitely drummed into you, all kinds of things I'd experience, the names I'd be called."[7]

It was not his style to fade into the background, however. Foxx was not disrespectful, but he did not let derogatory racial com-

Foxx warms up the crowd at a celebrity basketball game. In high school he was a star athlete, participating in football, tennis, and track.

ments keep him from standing out in the community. He played football on Friday nights, was in the Boy Scouts, and used his musical talent in church each week. He did not let racial issues affect the way he lived his life or the decisions he made. However, at the same time he could not pretend that racial issues were not there. Foxx states, "With me, the racial thing was a big thing. To be a strong black man in Texas, you were risking your own life."[8]

Gifted Athlete

Although the racial slurs bothered Foxx, his talent as an athlete gave him an additional layer of self-confidence. In high school, he played football and tennis and was a member of the track team. He was especially good at football, playing varsity quarterback and passing for more than one thousand yards his senior year. In Texas, where the sport was extremely popular, he attained the status of local hero. As many as fifteen thousand fans would pack the local stadium on a Friday night to watch the Terrell Tigers play. Their cheers gave him his first taste of success. "You feel like you're a star in your own town because Texas is all about football," he said years later, as he looked back on his playing days. "Our whole town would stop on Friday to come see what we were doing out there on the field. I have dreams sometimes of going back to the field, replaying some of the games we lost. It was a great experience."[9]

Although the fans cheered Foxx on when he made a stellar play, they also were not shy about letting him know when he made a mistake. Even Foxx's pastor would "boo" him when he threw the ball out of bounds. During these football games, Foxx learned to perform under pressure.

Attracting Attention

Foxx could not deny that he had a certain magnetism that made people notice him. When he performed in a talent competition while he was in high school, women gathered around the stage to be close to him as he sang. Foxx was a natural leader, whether he was calling plays on the athletic field or directing the choir at his church. He was also a natural performer who could make his teammates laugh at his impersonations of their coach. Garnering attention was second nature for the talented Foxx.

Black performers of the day showed Foxx that success was possible in the entertainment field. Although his grandmother limited the type of music the family listened to at home, Foxx was allowed to watch television. While he was growing up, black comedians such as Flip Wilson, Redd Foxx, and Richard Pryor were nationally known through their performances in television series and movies. Seeing them showed Foxx that a black comedian had the potential for success. He had thoughts of becoming a performer, and in high school he and some friends started a rhythm and blues band called Leather and Lace. He also developed an after-school show called "An Afternoon with Eric Bishop." Even as a teen, he was naturally at the center of the action and was setting his sights on being a star.

Unnoticed

Foxx had no problem attracting the attention of his classmates, teammates, and the members of the church choir, but there were two people who seemed to be ignoring his accomplishments. Foxx had little contact with his birth mother and father. As a teen he hoped they would notice what he was doing with his life. However, they did not.

As he grew older, Foxx became increasingly hurt by his parents' lack of attention. He was a boy who loved to perform and expected to be noticed, and their lack of interest in all that he was doing both perplexed and stung him. "You know, I didn't need much. But just a little bit would have been, like, 'OK, at least you're checking for it,'" he said. "You know? At least you're checking on me." [10]

His grandparents loved him, supported him, and gave him a good home, but at the same time Foxx could not help but wonder why his biological parents remained so distant. He was a good student, a talented musician, and so good at athletics that his picture was in the *Dallas Morning News* because of his achievements in football. Yet his father never attended one of his football games. The absence of his mother, and especially his father, put a fire into Foxx to succeed and make people take notice of him. Years later he said, "That absence made me angry. It made me want to be something. I said, I'm going to make you look up one day and say, 'That's my son.'" [11]

Loss of a Loved One

The distant relationship he had with his birth parents was not the only painful part of Foxx's high school years. His grandparents were aging, and while his grandmother remained strong and healthy, his grandfather's health deteriorated. When Foxx was seventeen, he lost the man who had helped raise him since he was a baby.

It was Foxx who attempted to revive his grandfather as he lay dying in the middle of the night. He performed cardiopulmonary resuscitation (CPR) on him, but his efforts proved fruitless. The ordeal impressed upon Foxx the fleeting nature of life, as he realized how suddenly everything could change. "I'll

Comedian Richard Pryor was a role model for the young Jamie Foxx.

never forget doing CPR on him at about 3 in the morning and thinking that life and death are so close to each other," [12] he later said.

His grandmother now turned to her grandson for comfort and hope for the future. The experience, Foxx said, made him a man. "My grandmother looked at me," he recalled. "'What are we going to do? We're going to keep living. What else can we do?' So, it made me a man." [13]

Culture Shock

College in San Diego, California, was 1,400 miles (2,252 km) away from his home in Terrell, Texas, and Foxx's eyes were opened to a different part of the world when he left for school. In an interview with William Booth of the *Washington Post,* Foxx called himself "the original black Beverly Hillbilly": "I was on the beach in my shoes and my socks, going to the pay phone, calling my homeys, and saying, whoa, the water out here comes right to the edge of the land, just crazy."

College was also much more culturally diverse than his hometown. There were students from eighty-one different countries, which made racism less significant. Foxx was often the only American in his classes. "You'd be exhausted trying to be prejudiced because you wouldn't know who was what," he told Booth. "I'm looking at a guy like me—hey brother, he'd be speaking Spanish, he'd be from Italy or Africa or Venezuela."

During college in San Diego, Foxx appreciated the ethnically diverse campus and enjoyed the area's sunny beaches.

Looking for a Way Out

As his high school years came to a close, Foxx looked to a future that would take him away from Terrell. He loved his grandmother but believed he had little chance to make something of himself in his hometown. There were few job opportunities for him there. He and his friends admired people who were fortunate enough to get jobs in a photo shop for $8.95 an hour. He briefly considered staying in Terrell for love, but the girl he had his eye on was falling for someone else. He realized his best chance for success and happiness would come elsewhere.

The racism in Terrell also bothered Foxx. No matter how good an athlete he was, how well he played the piano, or how cleverly he could make people laugh, the racial slurs were always present. He was tired of hearing them and wanted to go somewhere where he would have more opportunities to put his many talents to use.

There was one more personal incentive for Foxx to leave. As hard as he had tried, nothing he had done in Terrell had gotten his parents' attention. He knew he could not achieve the success and fame he sought by staying in Terrell, so he looked for a way out.

Music Scholarship

As a teen, Foxx showed promise as an athlete, performer, and musician. Although Foxx's athletic talent was considerable—he became the first quarterback at his school to pass for more than a thousand yards—a college athletic scholarship would not be his way out of Terrell. Neither would his knack for comedy and impersonations, which he had used mainly to bring levity to his team's locker room and make his classmates break into laughter. Instead, he decided to use his musical abilities.

Foxx graduated from high school in 1986 and received a piano scholarship to U.S. International University in San Diego, California (in 2001 the school merged with another college to become Alliant International University). The university's students came from all over the world, and Foxx gladly accepted the opportunity to attend the school. He had big plans. He admired pop singer and entertainer Lionel Richie and wanted to emulate his career as a performer. Foxx envisioned a future onstage as a popular rhythm and blues singer and pianist.

From Music to Comedy

Working toward his goal of becoming a professional musician, Foxx studied classical music in college for several years. Although he also played drums and trumpet, his talent on the piano had won him the scholarship and that was the instrument he concentrated on. In college, Foxx encountered a world that was very different from the life he had left behind in Terrell. He studied and learned with people from all over the world. His classes included a piano course taught by a Russian instructor and a music class taught by a teacher from Yugoslavia. The students had varied cultural backgrounds, and the atmosphere at the school was free of racism.

Although his scholarship paid for his schooling, Foxx still needed to earn extra money. He got a job playing piano for the school's dance classes, earning $16 an hour.

Performing was on his mind as he studied at college. He dreamed of becoming a rhythm and blues singer and pianist and landing a record deal. On weekends he and his girlfriend would drive to Los Angeles to try to meet people in the record industry who might help him realize his dream.

It was the Los Angeles comedy scene, however, that would make more of a mark on his future. He and his girlfriend would visit the city's comedy clubs, and seeing the other comedians perform rekindled Foxx's interest in doing impersonations. Even when they went to dance clubs, Foxx would take the microphone onto the dance floor and entertain the crowd with impersonations.

College was difficult for Foxx, and gradually his attention drifted away from his studies. His dreams of being a professional musician were put aside one night in 1989 when his girlfriend dared

Taking the Stage

Foxx's first comedy performance at the Comedy Store on an open mike night in 1989 included impersonations of some well-known entertainers. The ease with which he impersonated them convinced him to turn to comedy as a career. "I went on as Cosby, Cosby the gangster," the performer recalled in a story by Josh Tyrangiel in *Time* magazine in 2004. "I did Tyson. I did Reagan. When I got on that stage I felt like all the elements were finally in place. It was so easy."

In another interview, Foxx recalled how the performance made him feel and made his future clear. "It was the most incredible feeling," he told interviewer Cynthia True for *Texas Monthly* in 1998. "It was. 'Okay, I think I know what I want to be right now.'"

In 1989 Jamie Foxx began performing stand-up comedy at a club like this one.

him to go onstage during open mike night at a club called the Comedy Store. Open mike (microphone) night gave unknown comedians the chance to go onstage and try out their material, to see if they had what it takes to pull off a comedy act in front of an audience. Accepting the dare, Foxx stepped in front of the audience. He impersonated comedian Bill Cosby, boxer Mike Tyson, and President Ronald Reagan. The audience loved his performance, and Foxx began to think about a career in comedy. He was comfortable being onstage, it was easy for him to get laughs, and comedy satisfied his desire for attention.

In 1990, after three years of study, Foxx left the university. He had a new goal in life—becoming a professional comedian. When he was younger, it looked as if his talent in athletics or music would define his future. Instead, it was his talent for impersonating others that would carry him forward. The skill had always been there, as evidenced by the second graders who minded their teacher for a chance to hear him tell jokes and the teammates who loved his impersonations of their coach. Now he was moving to Los Angeles to see if this innate ability would translate into a viable career.

Chapter 2

A Career in Comedy

Foxx had no training in comedy, just an ability to do uncanny, dead-on impressions of celebrities. He did not let his inexperience keep him from trying to break into the lineups at area comedy clubs, however. The hours Foxx had spent at the keyboard had taught him that the way to get better at something was to practice. Now, instead of practicing at the piano, he practiced his comedy performance many times. He dedicated himself to learning all he could about making people laugh.

Amateur Nights

Foxx's first step toward getting noticed as a performer was to move to Los Angeles in 1990. The city had a thriving comedy club scene, and its comedy venues provided Foxx with the best chance of appearing onstage. The city's clubs were where agents and television producers often looked for new talent.

Foxx had been rewarded with the crowd's applause the first time he appeared onstage at an open mike night, but one performance would not make his career. Foxx had to continue to look for opportunities to perform. Most of the comedy clubs held amateur nights where ordinary people could go onstage and perform. Foxx hoped to use amateur night as a way to develop and polish his comedy skills.

Foxx consistently attended amateur nights, hoping to be chosen to appear onstage. He would add his name to a list of aspiring comedians who wanted to perform, and the club manager would select those who would be asked to go onstage. There were usually more people who wanted to perform than there were slots available, and Foxx was not always chosen. He did not give up, however, and was out there seven nights a week trying to get noticed. He made only $25 a night—if he was paid at all for his appearance. Sometimes amateurs were paid, and other times they performed for free in exchange for the opportunity to appear in front of an audience and work on their material. It was not easy work. The crowd expected to be entertained and let performers know it. Although he was not making a great deal of money and ran the risk of being embarrassed in front of a room full of people, the potential for applause kept Foxx motivated. "Doing standup in L.A. is like being a gunslinger," he said. "But the first time you go on and you get the first laugh . . . you're good, because you have something to say." [14]

Staying Focused

Paying jobs as a comedian were scarce, however, and it was difficult to break into a comedy club's lineup and consistently appear onstage. Initially Foxx performed for free or for very little pay, and to support himself he had to work elsewhere during the day. He took day jobs selling shoes and working as a janitor, but he never lost sight of why he was in Los Angeles.

Foxx realized that he would have to push himself in order to win success in his new career. He saw others who were also trying to make it in the business but were lured away from a dedication to performing by the temptation to lounge on the beach or spend time with their friends. He did not openly criticize others who were less dedicated, because he did not want to attract undue attention or pressure from other performers by being arrogant about his dedication to his work. He was not in a race with other performers and did not compare his career to theirs, but he continued to push himself to do the best he could. "You just have to hope that the decisions you're making are going to push you—not in front of other people, because it's not a race, but to do great work," he said. "It's always good to be stealthy about it because then you don't have the pressure." [15]

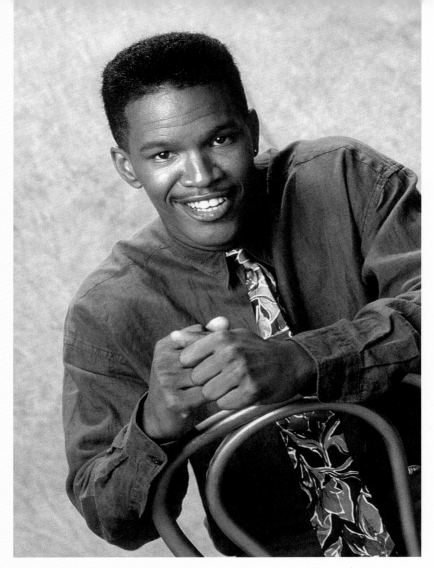

In his early years in Los Angeles, Jamie Foxx worked hard for little pay in order to break into the comedy club scene.

Becoming Jamie Foxx

Foxx was ready and willing to go onstage every night, but he was not always chosen to perform. After he had been doing his impressions at comedy clubs for a while, he began to suspect that he was too talented for his own good. He figured that some club owners kept him offstage on purpose because when he made it onstage

Humor in His "Sole"

In order to make money to live on while he tried to get work as a comedian, Foxx took other jobs. One of these jobs was as a salesman in a shoe store. Even when working at his day job, however, he never completely let go of comedy.

When he was helping customers at the shoe store, Foxx would entertain them with goofy banter. He would offer to bring a woman a size 9 shoe, even when he knew she wore a size 10. "I would bring out a size 9 and a 10 and maybe a little bit bigger," he told interviewer Ed Gordon for *CBS News*. "She says, 'What is wrong with this shoe, it's——'[I'd say,] 'Listen, it's probably European.'"

he was upstaging some of the favored performers. "If you get the name around too much and you're actually funny, they try to keep you from going up,"[16] he commented.

In order to get more time onstage, he came up with a plan. He had been performing under his birth name, Eric Bishop. With that name he was not getting called onstage as often as he would have liked, however, so he decided to sign in at the comedy clubs under a stage name.

When deciding which name to use, he thought of another tactic that would help him get chosen by club owners. He noticed that there were few female comics on the list waiting to perform and they were usually chosen to go onstage because the club owners wanted to break up the monotony of male performers. To increase his chances of having his name called, he made up unisex names. One of these names was Jamie Foxx. "I felt that a unisex name like Jamie or Tracy would be better because that way the audience wouldn't know what to expect," he said. "And I just liked Foxx with two xx's."[17]

One night at the Improv in Santa Monica, a highly respected comedy club, Foxx signed in for the chance to be a filler performer while an HBO special was being taped. To increase his chances of being selected, he used the name Jamie Foxx. His plan worked, and the announcer, expecting a woman to answer when the name Jamie Foxx was called, was surprised when a male voice replied. Foxx took the stage, and the audience responded appreciatively to his impersonations of Tyson and Reagan. That night he proved in front of an impressive crowd that he could make an audience laugh. His performance sent him on his way as a professional performer.

From then on, Foxx was known professionally as Jamie Foxx. He was not ashamed of being Eric Bishop, but the name Jamie Foxx had gotten him onstage when it counted and looked as if it could take him to the next level in his career. He likened it to going from an ordinary citizen to a superhero. "Eric Bishop is Clark Kent and Jamie Foxx is Superman," [18] Foxx said.

Comedy Champ

Foxx continued to work his way up the comedy ladder, performing as often as he could around the state. In 1991, after about eight months of doing stand-up, he entered and won the Bay Area Black Comedy Competition in Oakland, California. The competition, founded in 1987, showcased urban comedy.

Foxx was beginning to attract attention and was even noticed by some of the celebrities he was impersonating. He got to know Mike Tyson after Tyson saw him doing his impersonation of the boxer at a small comedy club. Rather than being upset by Foxx's act, Tyson was impressed by it and would call for the impersonation whenever he saw Foxx.

Foxx's career soon got a boost when he began working with managers Jamie and Marcus King. They worked in the entertainment industry and helped him plan his career moves. With Foxx's reputation and the Kings' assistance, Foxx found new opportunities that would take him beyond the comedy club stage. Soon he was going to auditions for television shows.

It was a natural step for Foxx to take his career to television. He did not think of himself as a true comedian who got laughs by telling jokes, but as a performer who was extremely adept at getting laughs by doing impressions. He noted in a story in *Ebony* magazine by Aldore Collier that he held his microphone like Eddie Murphy and did gestures like Richard Pryor, yet he could not see himself doing stand-up comedy for the rest of his career. So when he was given an opportunity to stretch his performing ability to television, he took it.

In Living Color

There was one television show Foxx felt would fit his talents perfectly. *In Living Color,* starring brothers Keenen Ivory Wayans and Damon Wayans and their siblings, was an edgy show of sketch comedy that began airing nationally in 1990. The first time he saw *In Living Color,* Foxx had to turn the television off. He loved what he was seeing and could not stand not to be part of it. "I was like, 'It's killing me that I'm not on this show! I can't watch it!'"[19] he said.

Foxx has a knack for impersonating celebrities, including the boxer Mike Tyson (center).

Foxx portrays Ugly Wanda, a character he developed for In Living Color, *the show that helped him break into television.*

When the show put out a casting call and held auditions for another cast member, he tried out, along with many other performers. Foxx's talent stood out, however, and he was chosen as the newest member of the ensemble cast in 1991. Even after he began regularly appearing in the show's skits, Foxx did not

Starstruck

Before he became a well-known performer and had a chance to meet other celebrities on a regular basis, Foxx was as starstruck as anyone when he saw a popular performer in person. An outgoing person, he did not hold back when he saw someone he wanted to talk to. Foxx once saw actor Denzel Washington walk out of a theater in Los Angeles and marched right up to him. "I was like, 'Denzeeeeellll! Denzeeeelll!'" Foxx recalled in an interview with Oscar nominees for *Newsweek* years later. "I remember he put his elbow out, going, 'Hold on, hold on.'" After Foxx became a star himself, remembering that experience made him more understanding of fans who wanted to meet him. Having once been a fan himself, he knew what it was like to be in awe of a performer.

Having idolized actor Denzel Washington (pictured), Foxx is understanding of his own starstruck fans.

abandon his stand-up comedy career. There he created characters that he brought to *In Living Color.* One of these was a female character called Ugly Wanda. He got the idea for the character one night when he ran out of material when he was onstage in Atlanta. Thinking quickly, he asked all the good-looking women to clap their hands. Then he asked all the ugly women to start clapping. When that line brought laughter from the audience, he knew he had succeeded.

Ugly Wanda, whom Foxx played dressed as a woman, became a popular recurring character in the *In Living Color* sketches. Never realizing how ugly she looked, Wanda told potential dates, "I'm gonna rock your world!" Foxx said her appeal came from his ability to give her emotions. Although she had a comical physical appearance, she was not just a character to be laughed at and made fun of by others: She had feelings and could be sad at times. He gave the character some depth, although he played her for laughs.

In Training

In Living Color proved to be a great training ground for Foxx. The weekly show taught him how to pace himself when working with other comedians and gave him the opportunity to learn from its talented cast members. He felt comfortable on the set, as his gift for imitating people allowed him to easily climb into the skin of the characters he created. In addition, sketch comedy came as naturally to him as making his high school friends laugh. However, he did not think that he was in any way an expert at his craft. Costars Jim Carrey, Damon Wayans, and Keenen Ivory Wayans had so much more experience as comedians. "Keenen Ivory Wayans blew my mind," Foxx said. "He was definitely the principal and I was definitely the student, and he definitely let me know that."[20]

Foxx curtailed his dynamic personality on the set, quietly observing the other actors. During the show's rehearsals, Foxx would intentionally hold back on the lines he was developing for the skits. He did not want to deliver his most clever lines during rehearsal and risk losing the spontaneity that would bring laughs during the taping. He decided to showcase his best material when it mattered most.

Capturing More Roles

During this time, Foxx continued to audition for other television roles. In 1992, he earned a supporting role on the television series

Roc, a comedy on Fox starring Charles S. Dutton as a Baltimore garbage collector coping with his family and neighbors. In 1992 and 1993, Foxx appeared in several episodes as Crazy George, the neighbor of the main character.

In addition to working in television, Foxx also looked toward the big screen to further his career. His first role was a small part as a toy company employee in the Robin Williams film *Toys,* which was released in 1992. Sure of his onscreen ability, Foxx took the comedy techniques he was using on television and brought them to the film. He thought he was doing a great job of acting while he was making the movie, but when he saw himself onscreen he felt embarrassed. He realized that he had played the part in an animated fashion that came across too boldly. The comedy techniques he used on the television show

In 1992 and 1993, Foxx (left) played Crazy George in several episodes of the TV comedy Roc.

were too broad for the big screen, which demanded a more subtle performance.

Enjoying Success

Foxx was still a rookie performer, but his rapid rise from shoe salesman to comedy champ to actor surprised even the confident young man. He was amazed how quickly his life changed. "I went from going to college on a music scholarship and playing modern jazz for the dance class, where I was making sixteen dollars an hour, to Los Angeles doing jokes," he said. "And the next thing you know, I was making thousands of dollars a week."[21]

Despite his miscue in his first movie, Foxx had no reservations about taking advantage of the access to Hollywood parties and clubs that his career in television and comedy gave him. He would stay out all night, going to work at *In Living Color* the next day in the same clothes he had on the day before. He would cash his checks and go out on the town with thousands of dollars in cash in his pocket. He did not bother to keep close track of his money and once found in his closet a check for $48,000 that he had forgotten to cash.

His costars on *In Living Color* tried to restrain the freewheeling Foxx. They questioned his all-night partying and the way he was taking advantage of his success. Foxx, however, was so excited to be on television and so enthralled with his popularity that he paid them little attention.

"Fame Face"

Not every evening was an all-night party, however. Foxx still performed on area comedy stages, and now that he was recognized for his work on *In Living Color* he no longer had to fight for a spot in the night's lineup of comedians. However, now that it was easy for him to get onstage, Foxx began to reduce the amount of preparation he did for his act. He did not work on new stand-up routines or characters, but relied on his reputation and what he had already accomplished. His stand-up routine now lacked the edginess it had when he was first performing.

Foxx realized this one night when, after his show, another young comedian came onto the stage. From backstage, Foxx heard the crowd's laughter and hearty applause. Foxx's managers, Jamie and Marcus King, pointed out that if the audience continued to respond this way, the new performer was going to be a better comic than Foxx.

The newcomer's performance was a wake-up call for Foxx. He realized that he was not nearly as funny as the newcomer because he had put on what he would later call his "fame face." He had lost touch with his audience because he was too busy being famous to work on his craft and stay tuned in to what was making people laugh. "I had to go back to the comedy gym, you know, and get my thing back," he said, "because I'd gotten that fame face." [22]

New Direction

Foxx regrouped and rejuvenated his stage act. The revitalized act and his staple characters such as Ugly Wanda earned him his own HBO concert special in 1993. It included imitations of Michael Jackson, Prince, and Mike Tyson. Filled with adult-oriented humor, it was called *Straight from the Foxxhole*.

His career in television and stand-up comedy brought Foxx modest fame and a large circle of friends to party with until 1994, when *In Living Color* was canceled. Suddenly, many of the "friends" he had enjoyed going to parties with disappeared. They had enjoyed hanging around with him when he was on television, but once he lost that status they no longer bothered to get in touch. Foxx moved to Las Vegas, which seemed more similar to Texas than California had been, and found that few acquaintances called. "I'll never forget moving to Las Vegas and I didn't have any phone calls," [23] he said. Foxx rented an apartment in Las Vegas, although he kept a home in California as well. Without a television show to return to, Foxx had some decisions to make. He definitely wanted to continue performing, and stand-up was still an option.

Impressing His Friends

After Foxx began making money on *In Living Color,* he drove back to Terrell, Texas, to show off his success to his friends. He wanted them to be impressed by the car he was driving but did not think his 1979 Triumph TR7 was quite impressive enough. He wanted his friends to think he had really made it big, so he made a little adjustment to the car's paint job. "I painted over the insignia, so nobody knew what kind of car it was," he said in *Interview* magazine. "They were like, 'Is that a Ferrari?' And I'd say, 'Yes, yes—it's a baby Ferrari!'"

A few years later, after *In Living Color* was canceled, Foxx realized how nice it could be not to worry about impressing people. He got an apartment in Las Vegas, and one of the reasons he liked the city was that he did not have to worry constantly about what other people thought. To him, Las Vegas seemed similar to the town where he had grown up. "Vegas is a little like Texas," he told reporter Cynthia True for a November 1998 story in *Texas Monthly.* "It's a desert, it's hot. When you just want to live a regular life, being in Vegas is more regular. You'll actually see a 1979 Monte Carlo or a Grand Prix. Out in L.A., everyone has to have the latest thing."

He also continued to audition for more movie roles and had hopes of one day returning to television on another show. However, with stand-up comedy and television experience under his belt, he now also wanted to return to music, the talent that had given him his first chance at success.

Chapter 3

Pursuing All Options

After *In Living Color* ended, Foxx rekindled his love for music. He had sometimes used his musical talent in his comedy routine, imitating Ray Charles playing the *Brady Bunch* theme on the piano or playing other songs at the end of his stage act. However, until now he had not pursued a career as a recording artist. Years earlier, when he was studying piano in college, he had visited Los Angeles with his girlfriend and dreamed of landing a record deal one day. Those dreams faded after he experienced success on the comedy stage, but now his musical ambitions were revived.

In 1994, he finally landed a recording deal. Fox/RCA records produced Foxx's first CD, called *Peep This*. The CD allowed him to showcase his talent as a singer and a musician, but it was made on a small budget and the result did not generate critical notice or acclaim. The album managed to make it as high as No. 12 on *Billboard's* rhythm and blues chart and No. 78 on *Billboard's* album chart. The single "Infatuation" was released and cracked the top 100, peaking at 92.

This first attempt at a musical career did not cause the same stir, or bring him as much money, as his work on the comedy stage. He had fulfilled his goal of being paid to make a CD, but its release did not earn him a reputation as a musician. Because he loved music, it would remain an important part of his life, but for his career he decided to return to comedy.

Fatherhood

Foxx was not ready to settle down, professionally or personally. He kept a firm grip on his career and also returned to the partying lifestyle he had cultivated. Long-term relationships with women were not part of his lifestyle. He dated many different women and commented that he did not see the value of getting married.

At the 2005 Academy Awards ceremony, Jamie Foxx poses on the red carpet with his daughter, Corrine.

His relationship with one of these women resulted in his fathering a daughter, Corrine. She was born in 1995, but the name of her mother was not publicly released and Foxx did not discuss her in the media until she was almost ten years old. She and her mother eventually moved a few blocks away from a home Foxx had in Tarzana, in California's San Fernando Valley. This allowed him to see his daughter more often. He still felt the pain of his parents' rejection and did not want Corrine to have the same experience. Although he was busy with his career, he made time for his daughter.

Stand-Up and Auditions

Foxx continued stand-up comedy, traveling around the country doing hundreds of shows per year, and auditioned for movie roles as well. In addition, he hinted to audiences at his live performances that he had his own television show in the works. Even though the show was not yet in production, Foxx was trying to generate interest and create an eager audience for a show he wanted to get on the air. "I told everybody I was working on *The Jamie Foxx Show,* and that when it came out, I wanted them to tune in,"[24] he said.

Always one to be working on a number of career opportunities at the same time, Foxx also did some voice-over work for the animated series *C-Bear and Jamal.* The show was about the adventures of a ten-year-old boy who wants to grow up but is hesitant to give up his teddy bear, named C-Bear. Tone Loc and Arthur Reggie III did the voices of the main characters, and Foxx was one of a number of cast members who did additional voice work for the series.

Foxx continued to audition for movie roles as well, but he lost out for a part in *Jerry Maguire.* Foxx read with Tom Cruise at the audition but made a critical error when he prodded Cruise to say his line. After Foxx had said his line, Cruise paused. Not sure what Cruise was doing, Foxx told him that it was his line. Cruise looked up at Foxx and said that he knew it was his turn to speak. The part went to Cuba Gooding Jr. instead of Foxx, and Gooding eventually won an Oscar for Best Supporting Actor for the role.

Foxx auditioned for a role opposite Tom Cruise in the film Jerry Maguire, but lost out to Cuba Gooding Jr. (left).

Foxx did land a minor role in the romantic comedy *The Truth About Cats and Dogs*. The movie, released in 1996, received average reviews and some praise for comedian Janeane Garofalo, who had one of the major roles. Foxx's role as Ed was such a minor one that he was not mentioned by name in the film's reviews. However, although the movie earned him little critical acclaim, it did keep him working.

That same year, Foxx kept his fledging movie career alive with a small role that reunited him with his *In Living Color* costar Damon Wayans. *The Great White Hype* was a satire about the boxing industry. In the film, Samuel L. Jackson played a boxing promoter trying to arrange a profitable fight for Wayans's character. Foxx's role as Hassan El Ruk'n was again a small one, and he received no individual critical acclaim for his performance. Reviewers had some positive things to say about the movie as a whole, however, even though it did not pull in large audiences.

"This rude satire of the fight game . . . doesn't quite deliver the expected knockout punch," wrote reviewer Michael Sauter. "But it does land enough sharp jabs to make it one of the best movies nobody saw this year."[25]

Return to Television

Foxx went from minor roles to a starring one when the television show he had hinted at in his stand-up act finally made it to the airwaves in 1996. The WB network picked up *The Jamie Foxx Show*, which he starred in and coproduced. Making the show required Foxx to put in fourteen-hour days on the set, but his efforts helped the show become one of the higher-rated ones on the WB network.

The Jamie Foxx Show marked a departure from Foxx's adult-oriented stage act. The family-friendly series mirrored Foxx's life and entry into show business. It featured Foxx as Jamie King, a

Snoozing Star

With a television show to make, a movie to promote, and songs to write, Foxx was driving himself to the point of exhaustion in the mid-1990s. He was so tired that when a reporter from *People Weekly* came to his house to interview him, Foxx dozed off while he was talking. "Maybe it's because the lights are low in his spacious San Fernando Valley home, or that the leather couch Foxx is sprawled across is just too cushy to keep him from lapsing into blank stares between words," mused writers Steven Lang and Marc Ballon in the article "Crazy like a Foxx" in the January 13, 1997, issue. "Even his dog Juice, angling for attention, can't rouse him." After a few seconds, however, Foxx's eyes flipped open and he resumed the interview.

Foxx relaxes on the set of **The Jamie Foxx Show,** *a family-friendly series that he starred in and coproduced.*

struggling performer from Texas who goes to Hollywood with the hope of launching his career. The parallel ended there, however, as the character Foxx played on television has difficulty launching a performing career and ends up working in his family's hotel, the King's Tower.

The cast included Garrett Morris, a comedian who had starred in *Saturday Night Live* in the 1970s and now played Foxx's uncle on the show. The character of Aunt Helen was played by Ellia English, while Christopher B. Duncan played the straitlaced Braxton P. Hartnabrig. Garcelle Beauvais played Fancy Monroe, a desk clerk who is Foxx's love interest on the show. During the series' five-season run, guest stars such as Kevin Garnett, Ice Cube, Mary J. Blige, and Gary Coleman made appearances on the show.

The show's plots generally revolved around King's attempts to jump-start his career and his infatuation with Fancy. Over the course of the show's run, his character becomes more and more successful in finding work and in wooing Fancy. However, he also has to learn to juggle work and his personal life when his commitment to his job intrudes on the time he's able to spend with his girlfriend.

Making People Take Notice

When he was not making new episodes for his show, Foxx became a one-man publicity machine for the program. He did not think the network was putting enough effort into promoting the show, so he did it himself. He pushed it relentlessly during performances of his stand-up act while he was on the road. "Some of the execs just don't get you, so they'll back off from you," he said. "They'll let a show die. They don't feel that African American shows are worthy of advertisement as far as white people are concerned."[26]

In his act, Foxx worked to broaden his appeal beyond a primarily black audience and learned to tailor his jokes to people of any background. In Dallas, in front of an audience that was primarily black, he made a joke about the attention paid to the death of Princess Diana, saying that she really was not a princess for black people. In cities with a primarily white audience, he changed the joke to say that she really was not a princess for Americans. He wanted to prove that he could appeal to audiences of any race. "I keep screaming [to network executives] at the top of my lungs, 'You don't understand! I've been to Boise, Idaho! I've been to Davenport, Iowa! Those people come out for me!'"[27] Foxx said.

Compromises

Although Foxx enthusiastically supported his show and put in long hours on the set, the final product was not as good as he would have liked. He wanted to make a funny show that people found special, but he realized that it was a mediocre product. Foxx was ambitious, however, and the show at least kept him employed and prevented his name from fading from the public's view.

In addition to working in television, Foxx continued to hold onto the hope that he would one day be considered a viable movie actor. He thought that the best way to achieve this goal was to continue working in any capacity. In order to be considered for a role in a major movie someday, he thought he should take as many minor roles as he was offered. However, the compromise he made by this method of career building was to be part of some low-quality films.

Foxx landed his first starring role in *Booty Call,* a 1997 comedy film aimed at black audiences that followed the antics of two friends during a double date. The movie was roundly criticized for its poor

Jamie Foxx's first starring role was in the movie Booty Call, *which was widely criticized for its lowbrow humor.*

attempts at humor (it included jokes such as naming Foxx's character Bunz). The movie also starred Vivica A. Fox, Tamala Jones, and Tommy Davidson. "Most of the time, the amiable foursome is left ambling aimlessly from one so-so sketch concept to the next: four characters in search of a comedy,"[28] wrote reviewer Mike D'Angelo.

The movie's poor quality and lowbrow humor raised the ire of comedian Bill Cosby, who was disappointed that a comedy aimed at black audiences would sink so low. "You talk to the guys putting that image out there and they'll say, 'Would you rather me be waiting in the alley for you or making *Booty Call*?' I say: 'Have you looked in the paper in the want ads?' . . . There is a middle ground and there is no need for a *Booty Call*."[29]

Foxx later admitted that when he was making the movie he knew it would not be good and that there was nothing artful about it. However, he noted that he had few choices if he wanted to continue to work. He likened the situation to playing basketball in a junior college before moving on to a larger school with a major program. "You gotta stay in the hunt," Foxx said, explaining his appearance in *Booty Call* and a later movie that also flopped, *Held Up*. "You say, 'Hey, our team is going to lose by fifty points, but I'm going to have ten rebounds, twelve assists and eight steals. If I keep my stats up, somebody is going to [notice].'"[30]

Moving Up the Ladder

Stand-up comedy also helped Foxx keep his name in front of audiences. During his eleven-month national tour that ended in 1998 and grossed almost $5 million, he entertained with daring impressions. He imitated Tupac Shakur and Biggie Smalls, rap stars who had been killed, as well as the politically active Jesse Jackson. His material also included bits about O.J. Simpson, the football star and actor who had been tried for murder and found innocent. The act also included singing, as Foxx blended his talent for music into his comedy routine.

Foxx continued to beef up his acting résumé with supporting roles in movies. In 1998 he edged away from comedies with a role in a movie that was a mixture of comedy and drama. *The*

Attentive Student

Doing imitations and making people laugh came easily to Foxx, and his skill for doing impersonations helped him in his acting. He could study people who resembled the characters he created onscreen and use their mannerisms in his portrayal. After making his first movie, however, Foxx learned that it was the subtleties of a character's personality that made a role come alive.

Foxx's first role was a small part in the movie *Toys*, which starred Robin Williams. When he saw himself onscreen, he quickly realized that he had played the role too broadly and had not done the little things that would have kept his character from being overwhelming onscreen. "I was just too animated," he told writer Elvis Mitchell in a 2004 article in *Interview* magazine. "I played this kid that was working for a toy company, and I was like, (raises voice) 'Yo man! I'm taking out the trash!' Just way too big."

Realizing that he was not as good an actor as he had thought he was, Foxx made a determined effort to improve by paying attention to how better actors carried off their roles. On *In Living Color,* he got tips by watching comic actors Damon Wayans and Jim Carrey. To teach himself how to act in movies, Foxx studied others who did it well onscreen. "I watched Denzel Washington. I watched Laurence Fishburne," he said in the 2004 *Interview* magazine article. "I watched Al Pacino. I learned how to act from watching movies."

Players Club was written and directed by rap star Ice Cube and gave Foxx the opportunity to work with comedian Bernie Mac. Mac had one of the top roles in the film about a Southern strip club, but Foxx was credited with having the funniest scene. He played a DJ who works at the club and falls in love with a stripper. The humor comes in when he then has to meet her father. The movie was shot for a relatively low budget of $4.5 million and for its production price did well at the box office, earning more than $8 million in its first weekend. Foxx's comedic turn as the DJ earned him some individual praise for his work, and he began to be noticed as an actor who could carry a scene. The movie marked a departure from pure comedy for Foxx as he continued to diversify his career.

Foxx had become adept at taking varied steps to keep his career moving forward. He answered the end of *In Living Color* by turning to music and then used his comedy to bring himself back into television. He continued to do stand-up to promote his TV show and took little steps with his movie career, using small roles and mediocre movies to keep his name from being forgotten. He moved gradually up the ladder, performing music, comedy, and drama, hoping to find the niche that would set him apart.

Chapter 4

Breaking Out

Foxx was using every performing talent he had to stay employed. He sang on his television show, took roles in comedies, and shifted his acting toward drama. His acting was beginning to attract some notice, but he had not yet managed to work his way into a major film.

There were a number of young black actors vying for the same roles Foxx was auditioning for, and he needed a way to set himself apart. Although comedy had taken him onstage and had been the mainstay of his television and movie career, he began to look at drama as a way to break out of the pack. He had never seen himself as a true comedian but as a skilled impressionist. His ability to mimic mannerisms and voices allowed him to get into character, and he would now try imitating serious characters as well as goofy ones.

Dramatic Turn

When Foxx looked around at his competition for comedy roles, he realized that he was up against other comedians who had turned to acting. Martin Lawrence, Chris Rock, and Chris Tucker all managed to be chosen ahead of Foxx for comedy roles. Will Smith, a rapper turned actor, also was ahead of Foxx in being selected for acting roles. It seemed to Foxx that all these performers had the ability to set themselves apart, but he still had to find his niche.

Tired of being offered parts only in low-tier comedies, Foxx turned toward dramatic films to increase his chances of being noticed. He attempted to break in not as a lead actor, but as a supporting member of the cast. This tactic would give him a better chance of being selected and also allow him to quietly absorb acting tips from the more experienced actors who had the lead roles.

Determined Audition

An opportunity for Foxx to audition for a dramatic role arose when director Oliver Stone was looking for an actor to play a quarterback in his 1999 movie about life in professional football,

After Foxx lost movie roles to Chris Rock (pictured) and other comedians, he began auditioning for serious dramas.

Any Given Sunday. Initially wanting someone who would be a big box office draw, Stone had his eye on rap star and producer Sean (Puffy) Combs. However, Combs did not work out for the part, so Foxx got his chance to audition for it.

Actually, Foxx first read for a different role in the movie. He auditioned for the part of a sports agent, which would have given him only a few lines. However, when he heard that Stone was still looking for someone to play the quarterback, Foxx quickly had his managers arrange another audition. He was not intimidated by auditioning before a powerful director for his first significant dramatic role. He would be able to put his athletic ability and high school football experience to use, in addition to the experience he had gained as an actor. He knew what it was like to play under pressure, and he knew how to throw a football.

The audition did not go as well as Foxx had hoped, however. Stone was initially critical in his assessment of Foxx's acting ability, saying it was not subtle enough for the movies. He told Foxx he was simply reading the lines rather than getting into the character. According to Foxx, Stone said, "I am not gonna waste one inch of film on you if you sit here and you're doing a monologue." [31]

Foxx was not deterred by Stone's assessment of his acting ability, however. He still believed he was right for the role and was determined to prove it to Stone. With the help of some friends, he made a mock training-camp video, starring himself as quarterback Willie Beamen. After seeing Foxx throw the football and act in the video, Stone was convinced. The video and Foxx's high school quarterbacking experience earned him a spot in the movie.

Taming His Ego

This film was at a different level than the movie work Foxx had done previously. It had a bigger budget and included a number of veteran actors as well as famous sports figures. Also notably, *Any Given Sunday* gave him the opportunity to work with an Oscar-winning director. Stone had earned Best Director awards for *Platoon* and *Born on the Fourth of July*. He had also directed actors James Woods, Willem Dafoe, Tom Cruise, and others in

Screamin' Beamen

When Foxx auditioned for director Oliver Stone for a role in the football movie *Any Given Sunday,* Stone asked Foxx if he could throw the football. Foxx claimed he could throw it 70 yards (64 m), and to prove it he put the throw on tape. Instead of a video of him just throwing the football, Foxx decided to impress Stone by turning it into a music video.

To pull it off, Foxx got six of his friends together to make a tape that showed what Beamen would have been like at training camp. The video included a catchy chant that Foxx had put together to show Stone that he understood the motivation of his arrogant character. He described the video in a story by Jane Sumner in the *Dallas Morning News*. "I got out of this Mercedes, got a Deion Sanders jersey on for the Dallas Cowboys and my helmet," Foxx said. "Music was playing, and I came up with this chant: 'My name is Willie Bea-men. I got the ladies scream-in.' So we put all this on a tape and cut it down to four minutes."

Oscar-nominated performances and had directed *Wall Street,* which earned an Academy Award for Michael Douglas.

Foxx would be working with an elite group of actors on the set of *Any Given Sunday.* Oscar-winning actor Al Pacino got top billing as Tony D'Amato, the football team's harsh but faltering coach, while Cameron Diaz played the team owner. Woods, who had been a producer, actor, and director during a career that began in 1970, played the team doctor, and Charlton Heston was the football commissioner. The cast also included veteran actor Dennis Quaid, rap star LL Cool J, and hard-hitting Lawrence Taylor, who had been a feared linebacker with the New York Giants, as well as Ann-Margret, Lauren Holly, Elizabeth Berkley, and football legend Jim Brown.

With all the talent around him, Foxx knew he needed to set his ego aside when he entered the movie's set. He had been successful in television and comedy with outgoing and flamboyant characters, but he had not equaled that success in movies. As when he first joined the cast of *In Living Color,* Foxx again looked at himself as a student, while he considered the rest of the cast as his teachers.

Foxx wanted to impress upon Stone that he would be open to the director's suggestions. At the audition, when Stone mentioned that he was frustrated by spoiled actors, Foxx assured him that his ego would not interfere with his taking direction from Stone or from absorbing information from veteran actors such as Pacino. "When you meet someone and let them know you are a prepared student and not a fearful student it helps you," [32] he said.

In addition to absorbing information and tips from his costars, Foxx subtly sought out ways to engage them in conversation. During downtime on the movie's set, Foxx would chat with LL Cool J about rap music and ask Pacino to play chess. Throughout the chess match, Foxx would encourage Pacino to open up about his previous movie experiences. "He's pretty good, but I would let him win the majority of the games, because if you beat him, then you don't get a chance to stick around and hear all his stories," [33] Foxx explained.

Al Pacino and Cameron Diaz starred in **Any Given Sunday,** *a film in which Foxx portrays a football quarterback.*

Taking the Hits

To get into the character of brash young quarterback "Steamin'" Willie Beamen, who gets his break in the National Football League (NFL) when the two quarterbacks playing in front of him are injured, Foxx wanted to capture the self-assured attitude of NFL players who know they have talent and are not afraid to flaunt it. To do this he hung out with real, outspoken NFL stars, such as Ricky Watters, Keyshawn Johnson, and the flamboyant Deion Sanders. To balance his character's personality, he also spent time with quiet yet talented quarterback Warren Moon. On the movie's set, he spoke with Jim Brown, considered the best running back ever to play the game. Foxx took something from each of their personalities and wove it into his character's part.

Stone's film took a serious look at the NFL, and Foxx's athletic skills were an asset as he proved that he could both act like a quarterback and play like one. While making the movie, Foxx took some hard hits from 200-pound (91kg) defenders rather than relying on a stunt double. Although the movie was a painful one to make, he was proud of his work in it and Stone was impressed by his attitude. "I can't say he did all his own stunts, but he did more than he had to and took a pounding," Stone said. "That exemplifies his drive as an actor and athlete." [34]

Foxx got so immersed in his role that a scripted argument between his character and the one played by LL Cool J turned into a real fight. The scuffle surprised Foxx. "It was a real manly type set, a lot of testosterone, and I guess one of his testosterones broke," [35] Foxx later joked.

Opening Some Eyes

Any Given Sunday initially performed impressively at the box office, taking in more money on its first weekend than any of Stone's previous movies had, but the movie was disappointing to many fans and critics and was criticized for its rough style. Stone's technique, which included scenes of Foxx talking interspersed with scenes from the movie *Ben Hur,* was deemed a distraction. "The trouble with the movie is its style, all handheld shots and short,

In Any Given Sunday, Foxx worked alongside such top veteran actors as Dennis Quaid (left) and Al Pacino (right).

jagged cuts," wrote reviewer Richard Schickel in *Time*. "They're supposed to represent the barely controlled anarchy of the sport (and to let Stone touch on far too many narrative points). But almost three hours of this jitter deteriorates from bravura film-making to annoying mannerism, and *Any Given Sunday* ends up less than the sum of its many, often interesting parts."[36]

Although the movie itself was a disappointment, Foxx's role as Beamen opened people's eyes to his talent as a dramatic actor. He surprised people with his portrayal of the quarterback. "Foxx gives a winning, charismatic turn in *Sunday*," [37] reviewer Allison Samuels wrote in *Newsweek*, adding that until now Foxx had been known mainly for his work in light comedies such as his television series and *In Living Color*. With his successful role, he added another dimension to his reputation as a performer.

Winning Stone Over

Director Oliver Stone initially questioned Foxx's acting ability, but Foxx won him over with his portrayal of quarterback Willie Beamen. A few years later, after Foxx had received an Oscar, Stone wrote a *Time* magazine article in which he praised Foxx for his work in *Ali* and also for the way he moved, sang, and played the piano in *Ray*. "Jamie Foxx was born to act," Stone wrote. "What is unique about Jamie is his uncanny ability to imitate . . . I told him one day he has to play James Brown. Who else would have the energy to pull that off?"

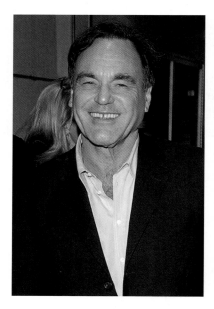

Director Oliver Stone has praised Jamie Foxx's acting ability.

Career Holdup

Foxx also wrote, produced, and performed the title song "Any Given Sunday" for the movie's soundtrack. This did not provide him with any additional opportunities to further his music career, however, just as his work with Stone did not guarantee him a continuous lineup of high-class film fare. Although he wanted to make better pictures, Foxx realized that in order to keep working he had to take advantage of the offers that came his way.

When comedian Rob Schneider dropped out of the comedy *Held Up* soon after filming began, Foxx took the lead role. He played a slick, charismatic character named Michael who must deal with a series of mishaps after stopping at a gas station with his girlfriend in a remote part of Arizona. After his girlfriend gets in a fight with him and leaves, his car is stolen and then three hoods try to hold up the gas station. When the police arrive, Michael is held hostage in the gas station.

While the movie allowed Foxx to display his talent at moments, it was held back by its lackluster style of comedy. "*Held Up* is a shoddy vehicle for Jamie Foxx to ride into the summer season on," wrote reviewer Robert Koehler. Koehler criticized the movie for its weak plot and for basing its stale humor on situations that put a black man into a white world. "Foxx can hardly be blamed for the poor results," Koehler said, "but he is also not the dazzling presence that defines star power—precisely what this creaky silliness needs." [38]

His next movie, *Bait,* in 2000, was no better. Foxx played a petty criminal going after a criminal mastermind, but the movie's plot did not hold viewers' interest. "Foxx has yet to find a starring big screen vehicle custom fit for his considerable comic range and potential dramatic appeal," wrote reviewer Dennis Harvey. The movie was "mindlessly diverting popcorn fare that's deleted from the viewer's hard drive before the final credit crawl," [39] Harvey wrote.

Leaving Television

These light comedies did not have the prestige of *Any Given Sunday* and did little to further Foxx's acting reputation. He was not yet an actor who had the ability to make a movie rise above a weak script. However, the films did allow Foxx to continue working and kept his name from fading from the spotlight.

Foxx needed to take whatever steps he could to stay working, as his television show ended its five-year run with its hundredth episode in 2001. The show wrapped up its plot lines by having Foxx's character, Jamie King, marry Fancy Monroe. The series finale was filled with big-name guest stars. Gladys Knight played Foxx's mother, and Marilyn McCoo and Billy Davis Jr. played Fancy's parents.

Foxx had mixed feelings about how the show had fared over the years. While he was happy that the program had lasted for five years on the air, he realized that its quality was not always high. The work Foxx did in television turned out to be a valuable training ground for him, however. Director Oliver Stone later pointed to the work Foxx had done on television as preparation for his movie roles. "It was in his TV training that he found his confidence and rhythm,"[40] Stone said.

As the show neared the end of its run, Foxx kept his options open. He talked of landing a new recording contract and returning to television with a Flip Wilson–style variety show, the type that featured a monologue, skits, and guest stars and had the edginess of *In Living Color.* In addition, he continued to audition for movie roles and made the short comedy *Date from Hell* with actress LisaRaye, who had worked with him in *The Players Club.*

Although he was an actor who always wanted to stay busy, Foxx hoped he could find better roles than the ones he had played in his most recent comedies. He was offered a script for a movie called *The Next Hot Negro,* which he turned down. He had success with a stand-up comedy tour and as the host of various awards shows, including the 2000 MTV Movie Awards, the MTV Video Music Awards in 2001, and the First Annual BET Awards that same year. Work was coming his way, and since he could be choosier than he had in the past, he did not want to settle for low-quality movies. He wanted to return to movies at the level of *Any Given Sunday.* He got his chance in a movie about the life of boxer Muhammad Ali, thanks to the work he had done in *Any Given Sunday* and the support he received from actor Will Smith.

"Float Like a Butterfly"

The movie *Ali* would be Foxx's next shot at success in a high-profile film. Director Michael Mann was familiar with Foxx from his work in *Any Given Sunday* and *In Living Color,* which helped Foxx secure a meeting with the director. Will Smith, who had the title role, was present when Mann and Foxx met. Smith wanted Foxx to have the supporting role of Bundini Brown, Ali's friend and cornerman. Mann, however, was not convinced that Foxx could carry the part.

Mann conceded that Foxx had talent, but noted that Foxx did not look anything like the balding, heavy Brown. Smith pressed Mann to include Foxx in the movie, however, and Mann finally agreed but let Foxx know that he had better step into the role effortlessly. The role of Brown was pivotal, as Brown was Ali's close friend who supported the boxer during his career and coined the famous phrase "Float like a butterfly, sting like a bee" to describe Ali's boxing style.

In Ali, Will Smith (center) portrays heavyweight boxer Muhammad Ali, while Foxx plays Ali's friend and cornerman, Bundini Brown. Foxx diligently studied Brown's mannerisms in preparing for the role.

Hey, Carlton

Foxx traveled to Africa with actor Will Smith to film scenes for the movie *Ali*. While Smith was recognized there, Foxx was not a familiar face to the African people. When Foxx and Smith arrived at the set, a large crowd was gathered, waiting for the actors. Smith was immediately recognized, but no one was certain who Foxx was.

Because he was with Smith, the fans assumed he was Carlton, a character on Smith's show *The Fresh Prince of Bel-Air*. A wave of embarrassment rippled over Foxx as he heard the crowd calling him the wrong name. "Like, 16,000 people started calling me Carlton," Foxx said in a 2002 *Teen People* article that listed "Star Woes: Their Most Embarrassing Moments."

Foxx put his heart into the role, studying videotapes to get his impersonation of Brown (who had died in 1987) just right. To make sure he had Brown's mannerisms down correctly, Foxx called Muhammad Ali and talked to him as Brown. Foxx knew he was on the right track when Ali started laughing, just as if he were chatting with his pal.

Foxx's efforts paid off: When the movie was released in 2001, he was praised for his performance, even though the movie itself did not meet the expectations of audiences and critics. Some reviewers noted that Foxx upstaged Smith as Ali. "Most of the supporting cast in *Ali* is overshadowed by the swaggering performances of ringleader Will Smith and Jon Voight as Howard Cosell," wrote reporter Jess Cagle in a brief *Time* article. "But if you look closely, you will see that the movie's most tragic and comic moments come from Jamie Foxx as Ali's cornerman, Drew (Bundini) Brown."[41]

Return to the Stage

After filming *Ali,* Foxx kept his stand-up skills sharp by performing around the country. The act he delivered was quite different
from the one he had used to break into show business more than
a decade earlier. Rather than humor about struggling to get by,
Foxx now used his experiences with other celebrities and his
movie costars as material for his stand-up act.

Foxx was now a recognizable actor and comedian rather than
a struggling performer. While some reviewers criticized him for
being out of touch with everyday people because of his increasingly affluent lifestyle, he still connected with his audience. Foxx
did not feel pressure to be funny, but saw comedy as something
that he enjoyed doing. "That's what I do," he said. "There's nothing in this world better than coming up with something funny."[42]

Foxx's act was taped for a comedy special, *Jamie Foxx: I Might
Need Security,* which aired on HBO in 2002. He also hosted and
coproduced a live comedy event, Laffapalooza!, America's Urban
International Comedy Arts Festival, which was presented in
Atlanta that year. The event was designed to help new comics get
the kind of exposure that Foxx had craved early in his career.

Star Billing

By 2002, Foxx was much more polished in his performance abilities and in his knowledge of how the entertainment industry
worked than when he had been a struggling comedian. Now that
he had a pair of solid dramatic performances behind him, it was
getting easier for Foxx to be accepted for movie roles.

However, Foxx concentrated on his stand-up career, rather
than movies, in 2002, touring the country with his act. The tour
gave him enough income so that he did not need to accept every
film offer that came his way, and he tried to be selective. However,
his first appearance after *Ali* did not generate much attention.

In 2003, Foxx returned to the big screen as one of the stars of
the movie *Shade.* The movie, which had an ensemble cast of big
names, including Sylvester Stallone and Melanie Griffith, capital-
ized on the popularity of poker. Foxx showed little of his comedic

side as he played a fast-talking gambler, recruited to play in a high-stakes game, who talks big and loses big. His character had a central role in the first part of the movie, but was absent from the movie's second half. The film received little notice, and Foxx continued to search for a decent role.

In 2002 Jamie Foxx hosts Laffapalooza in order to take a break from movies and focus once again on stand-up comedy.

Rule Breaker

After *Shade,* Foxx tried to coast through his next movie on his wit, and the result was an ill-conceived comedy that lacked new material. Foxx had a central role in *Breakin' All the Rules,* playing a jilted boyfriend who writes a best-selling book about breaking up. The movie did not have a detailed script, and Foxx and the other actors improvised most of their lines.

The movie tried to rely on identity mix-ups for laughs, but the result fell flat. One reviewer compared the movie's premise to the plot lines of romantic comedies of the 1960s. *"Breakin' All the Rules* breaks almost none as it recycles jumped-to conclusions and mistaken-identity twists from romantic comedies dating back to the Pleistocene Age of Doris [Day] and Rock [Hudson]," wrote reviewer Glenn Lovell. However, Foxx was not criticized as much as the movie was. Lovell gave Foxx credit for a diverse performance: "Foxx has returned to his comedy roots and demonstrates that he adroitly can juggle hip, horrified and hopelessly smitten."[43]

It was apparent that Foxx had talent, but he needed a movie with structure and a strong director to help him channel it. His persistence had paid off for him in the past, and Foxx continued auditioning. It was becoming clear that movie comedies were not the best direction for him, however. Although he still pulled in audiences with his stand-up act, his work in film comedies had not been kind to his career. Drama seemed an unlikely choice for the brash comedian, but that had been where he had excelled onscreen.

Foxx managed to bounce back from the failed movie by going after the opportunity of a lifetime—a role that would allow him to combine his talent for music, impersonation, and drama. When he heard that a biographical movie about music legend Ray Charles was being cast, he immediately put himself in the running for the lead.

Chapter 5

Dream Role

Foxx was now ready to make the film that would catapult his career to a new level. He had shown that he could adeptly juggle multiple facets of a career in entertainment. He had moved from stand-up comedy to television to movies, surprising critics with his turn as a dramatic actor. This previous dramatic work made it possible for him to be seriously considered for the lead in *Ray*, even though he had not taken the lead in a dramatic film before. His musical ability and talent for impersonation also came into play, as he would need to give a convincing portrayal of rhythm and blues genius Ray Charles. Before Foxx could think of taking his impersonation to the screen, however, he first had to convince Charles himself that he was worthy of portraying the revered singer.

The Director's Approval

The movie's director, Taylor Hackford, was inclined to back Foxx for the role. He had been impressed by Foxx's work in *Any Given Sunday* and *Ali*. In addition, Foxx looked enough like Charles to make his portrayal believable, and his piano-playing ability gave him the edge over other performers. When Foxx initially told Hackford that he played the piano, Hackford had responded that he, too, could play, but not like Charles. Then Foxx sat down at the keyboard, and the director realized the depth of Foxx's musical talent. He still did not know whether Foxx had the talent to carry the whole movie, but with his looks, musical talent, and solid dramatic performances, Hackford saw enough potential in Foxx to take a chance.

Hackford took a risk in selecting Foxx for the lead. Foxx had never been the linchpin of a dramatic movie before, and the comedies he had taken the lead in had failed miserably. Still, even though some people questioned the director's choice, Hackford was certain that Foxx could carry it off. "Nothing he had done was the size and scope of this," Hackford said. "But I was taken with the man and trusted my instincts."[44]

Pressure-Packed Audition

Foxx had received the approval of the director, but before securing the lead role he had to impress Ray Charles. Hackford arranged a meeting between the two men, and Foxx met Charles in a room where two pianos were sitting side by side. In this setting Charles would test Foxx's musical ability, as well as his tenacity.

Ray Charles (pictured) put Foxx through a vigorous piano audition before he agreed to let Foxx portray him in Ray.

Director Taylor Hackford works with Foxx on the set of
Ray. Hackford was impressed by Foxx's determination
and musical talent.

Charles put Foxx through a rigorous piano audition. Foxx was not scared as they played, but rather determined to prove that he could handle what was required. They played a variety of blues and gospel songs, including Charles's "Drown in My Own Tears" and "I Got a Woman," and Foxx managed to keep up with the talented musician.

Then Charles launched into a difficult piece by jazz artist Thelonious Monk. Not used to playing jazz, Foxx struggled, hitting the wrong keys and enduring criticism from Charles, who asked him how he could not hit the right notes when they were right under his fingers. The singer expected perfection.

As difficult as the piece was, Foxx did not give up. Rather, he worked at the piece for ten minutes, trying to find the notes that Charles kept telling him were there. Finally, Foxx understood the notes and he played to Charles's satisfaction. Once Foxx was able to play the piece, he got the part. Hackford was impressed by Foxx's determination, noting that Charles was testing Foxx as a man as well as a musician. "Ray got up, hugged himself and said, 'This is it! This kid's got it!'" Hackford recalled. "I watched Jamie grow to about 10 feet tall when Ray anointed him."[45]

Learning About Ray

Once he secured the part, Foxx wanted to do everything he could to make his portrayal of Charles realistic. He spent some time talking with Charles, but not too much. Charles was in his seventies when they met, but Foxx would be portraying him as a young man in the movie. Foxx wanted to capture not the personality of Charles as an older man, but the spirit and energy Charles had when his career was beginning.

To do this, Foxx talked to Charles's friends and relatives to get at the nuances of his personality. Foxx saw that Charles was a complicated man and knew that portraying him would mean figuring out how he acted in his home life, when he spoke with his children or talked on the phone, as well as onstage. He also watched Charles's taped performances and past interviews he had done. From listening to an interview on *The Dinah Shore Show*, a program that aired in the 1950s and 1960s, Foxx learned that Charles stammered when he was confronted with an uncomfortable question, and Foxx added that nuance to his portrayal. "I spent a year just watching Ray, I watched everything about him," Foxx said. "I watched him in person, and I spent days and weeks and months watching

Changing Because of Ray

Playing the part of Ray Charles changed the way Foxx approached life. Seeing how Charles used music to deal with what was happening around him, Foxx began writing more songs and bringing the musical side of his talent to the forefront. Foxx also noticed how Charles made the most of what he had every day. He admired Charles's determination and ability to keep pressing onward.

In an interview with Philip Wuntch of the *Dallas Morning News,* Foxx talked about how Charles shared his views on racial prejudice. Foxx said, "He just leaned back and told me, 'You're not gonna change those people. I can't see black and I can't see white, but I was met with bigotry all the time. I don't like labels. I don't call it rhythm and blues. I just call it music. And those magical notes change everything. You and me, we're not gonna be the ones that change people. But music is more powerful than people. It can change anything.'"

tapes of him. I studied everything I could about him, the way he ordered his food and the way he talked to his women. I let it all soak in."[46]

The role of Charles also demanded that Foxx learn all he could about the uncomfortable parts of Charles's life, such as his drug use and affairs with women. Although Charles was initially reluctant to discuss the affairs he had outside his marriage, Foxx eventually got him to open up about the women in his life. In addition to delving into the difficult side of Charles's life, Foxx also had to lose 33 pounds (15 kg) to look more like the lean musician. There were also piano riffs to learn, as Foxx needed to imitate Charles's musical style as well as his personality.

Big Responsibility

The role of Ray Charles was important for Foxx, not only because it was his first starring role in a major movie, but because he was portraying a black icon, and the black community in Hollywood wanted him to do it properly. This responsibility sometimes clashed with Foxx's interest in going out, staying out late, and having a good time.

Actor Will Smith reminded Foxx how important his role as Charles would be once when Foxx was just getting home from a party in the middle of the night. Foxx's friends had told Smith that he was out late. Smith went over to Foxx's house to impress upon him that he had better be in shape to take on the role of Charles. Foxx had been working out to lose weight and practicing the music he needed to learn for the role, but Smith wanted to make sure that Foxx was taking the role seriously. He said that everyone would be watching to see how the movie fared and he did not want Foxx to be at anything less than his peak. "You do not want to leave anything on the field,"[47] Foxx later said Smith told him.

In order to accurately portray Ray Charles, Foxx (pictured in Ray) observed the older man's habits and musical style and watched tapes of Charles's performances.

Blinded

Foxx took Smith's words seriously. As much as he liked to have a good time, he was diligent in his preparations for his role in *Ray* and serious when it came time to slip into character on the movie set. In addition to the preparations Foxx had done before filming began, he also had to learn what it was like to be blind. Charles had been blinded by glaucoma by age seven, and to realistically portray him Foxx wore special covers made for his eyelids that prevented him from seeing. While making the movie, he wore them all day long every day, an experience that was very uncomfortable for him at first. "I hyperventilated for the first week and a half," he said. "You feel like you're being closed up." [48]

Foxx had to rely on other people to assist him in getting around on the set. Although difficult, the experience of temporarily losing his sight helped him understand what Charles's world was

Trouble in New Orleans

Foxx's habit of heading out to a party after filming wrapped usually did not result in any problems, as he remained committed to his work and was a professional on the set. However, one night in April 2003, when Foxx was in New Orleans to shoot some scenes for the movie, he was involved in an incident at a New Orleans casino that resulted in his arrest.

The incident began after Foxx, his sister, and some others in their group were asked to show identification before going into the casino. Disagreements erupted. Foxx was eventually charged with battery for assaulting a police officer, the result of a fight he had gotten into while coming to the defense of his sister. He pleaded guilty to disturbing the peace, a misdemeanor, and was fined $1,500. He got a six-month suspended sentence and two years of probation.

like—what obstacles the musician had to overcome in order to achieve success and how the loss of his sight changed the way he perceived his surroundings. "After six hours of being blind you lose the sense of how a person is physically," Foxx said. "It was amazing to hear the little buzzing voices all around you." [49]

Impressive Performance

During the filming of *Ray*, there were signs that Foxx was doing a superb job with his portrayal of Charles. When Charles's children saw some scenes being filmed they had to leave the set because the performance was painfully realistic, and Foxx's costar Regina King said it felt like Charles was on the set. "I've never worked with anyone who has the ability to turn it on and off within a second," said King, who played Ray's backup singer, Margie Hendricks, in the movie. In the past King had also worked with Will Smith, Cuba Gooding Jr., and Eddie Murphy, and she called Foxx more talented. "He can literally be telling you a joke, then 'action,' and he would just fall into Ray." [50]

King was surprised by Foxx's dedication to the role. She knew him as a comedian, so she was not surprised that he was clever and smart, but she had not expected him to have such a respect for acting. Foxx also met Hackford's expectations, proving that the director had been right when he supported the rather untested dramatic actor in the lead role.

Because of Foxx's capable performance and his professionalism on the set, his after-hours activities were tolerated by the director. Hackford did not worry when he heard that Foxx was partying after filming ended for the day. "Whatever his kind of all partying style is, forget it. This is a man who is incredibly smart and who is totally committed," [51] Hackford said, adding that Foxx's "lust for living" helped him play Charles, who also liked to have a good time with his friends.

Waiting Game

Filming for *Ray* wrapped up in August 2003. It would be more than a year before it was shown in theaters, however, because

Hackford had to find a studio to distribute the film. The making of the movie had been financed by Phil Anschutz, owner of Crusader Entertainment, and other investors. Major Hollywood movie studios had been reluctant to partner with them on the project, so *Ray* was made without the backing of a major studio.

While the financing gave Hackford the means to make the movie, he and his backers could not get it out to theaters on their own. That required the connections of a major studio. To get the film before the public, Hackford made a rough cut of the movie and showed it to studio executives, asking them to take on the movie's distribution. He did not meet with immediate success. "[It being] an African-American biopic didn't help," Hackford said. "*Ali* did not make money. So they all turned it down." [52] The film was not picked up until February 2004, when Universal Studios agreed to take on the task of distributing it to theaters.

Redemption

While Hackford was shopping the movie to studios, Foxx began looking for more work. His work on *Ray* gave him the confidence to again try a different type of movie. "What Ray taught me is that when you rid yourself of excuses, there's nothing you can't do," [53] Foxx said.

His next step was to make a television movie with a message. Foxx was gaining clout as an actor, and he saw an opportunity to use his increasing celebrity to speak out about racial issues. To that end he made *Redemption: The Stan "Tookie" Williams Story*, which gave him a platform for speaking out about social injustice. The movie examined the life of Tookie Williams, the cofounder of the Los Angeles Crips gang, who was imprisoned and put on death row, where he became an anti-violence crusader and author. (He was executed in December 2005.) The role provided Foxx with an opportunity to talk about blacks and whites being sent to prison in uneven numbers.

Although criticized for failing to answer some questions about Williams's violent past, *Redemption* was another solid performance for Foxx. The movie was shown on the FX cable television station, and Foxx's performance generated positive reviews. "Foxx plays Williams with such coiled ferocity, you'll forgive *Redemption* its sins,"[54] wrote reviewer Marc Peyser.

Solid Reputation

While *Redemption* gave Foxx the chance to make a movie that supported a cause he believed in, his next film gave him the chance to forward his career. Foxx's reputation as a talented actor and hard worker won him a supporting role in *Collateral,* which starred veteran actor Tom Cruise. The movie was directed by Michael Mann, who had directed Foxx in *Ali*. Remembering the effort Foxx had put into his role as Bundini Brown, Mann chose Foxx to play a cabdriver who is forced to chauffeur hitman Cruise to his jobs.

His role as a "chatty cabby" driving Cruise around was vastly different from the types of roles that Foxx had played in the past. There was no comedy here, as there had been in his early movie and television roles. In his dramatic roles he had been a brash quarterback, a clever cornerman, and a musical genius. Now he needed to show his versatility as an actor by playing a cabdriver intimidated by Cruise.

Foxx exhibited his talent and versatility in the movie
Collateral. Here, he poses with director Michael Mann (left)
and fellow cast members Jada Pinkett Smith and Tom Cruise.

Foxx's ability to slip into such diverse roles and characters was made possible by his talent for impersonation. For his role in *Collateral,* he based the cabdriver on a friend who had nerdish tendencies. Cruise noticed the work Foxx put into perfecting his character and said that in turn Foxx pushed him to do his best in the movie. Foxx was a much more polished actor than he had been when he had failed the audition with Cruise for *Jerry Maguire.* He was comfortable and confident around the veteran actor, and Foxx and Cruise became friends while making the film. Foxx even joked that Cruise's association with Foxx would make the actor hipper. They got along so well that Cruise mingled with Foxx's friends at Foxx's thirty-sixth birthday party in 2003.

Although Cruise had been one of the top box office draws in the 1980s and 1990s and had been nominated for an Academy Award as Best Actor for his work in *Born on the Fourth of July,* in *Collateral* it was Foxx who earned the most praise. When the movie was released in August 2004, critics especially applauded Foxx's opening scene in which he chats with actress Jada Pinkett Smith, who plays a federal prosecutor. Their banter set the tone for the movie. "Foxx . . . makes what he does look effortless," wrote reviewer Steven Rea. "He's the reason to see *Collateral,* as he walks into the frame and walks off with the picture." [55]

He was also applauded for the interaction between him and Cruise. Their onscreen relationship was riveting when they walked the line between disdain and friendship. "Cruise and Foxx are so good together because they allow the two characters to get under each other's skin," wrote reviewer Owen Gleiberman. "They're buddies and enemies at the same time." [56]

Musical Moves

While Foxx was now having an easier time getting chosen for the movie roles he wanted, he was not one to let his other talents grow stale. His portrayal of Ray Charles had rekindled his interest in music. He wrote some songs and was able to join rappers Twista and Kanye West on the single "Slow Jamz," which became a No. 1 single for the three artists when it hit the top of the charts in February 2004. West sang the first verse of the song, while

Hosting the 2004 ESPY Awards gave Foxx further opportunity to showcase his talents for stand-up comedy.

Twista did the second and third. Foxx did the chorus. Foxx was included because West had spotted him singing on the *Any Given Sunday* DVD extras and had been looking for a song to perform with him.

To get a record deal of his own, Foxx had plans to impress long-time record producer Clive Davis. When Davis threw a Grammy party at the Beverly Hills Hotel in February 2004, Foxx arrived with Twista and West, musical artists he knew would help him get Davis's attention. Foxx did not want to be obvious about his desire for a record deal. When he performed that night as the evening's opening act, he did a new version of "Slow Jamz," which highlighted his piano playing and vocal skills. He later sang with Alicia Keys and Angie Stone. These performances were designed to make Davis notice Foxx's musical skill.

Foxx's plan worked, and Davis agreed to a record deal with Foxx. Foxx recorded a CD titled *Unpredictable* in 2005. Foxx felt confident that his new CD would be bigger than *Peep This*. "[That] was for limited money and for a small label," he said. "But we've got the heavy hitters on this one." [57]

The Laughs Keep Coming

In addition to his talent as an actor and musician, Foxx continued to showcase his ability as a stand-up comedian. At the 2004 ESPY Awards in July, he proved that he still had his comic edge. He generated laughs by serenading tennis star Serena Williams with a song he titled "Can I Be Your Tennis Ball?" Comedy allowed him to remind the entertainment world of his various talents and also kept Foxx sharp. "I looked out there and saw Cedric the Entertainer and Bernie Mac, and I said, 'Yeaaaah! Y'all thought I laid this comedy sword down!' If you get away from comedy, you forget what's going on out there," he said during an interview with an *Entertainment Weekly* reporter. "[With comedy], your mentality stays fresh." [58]

Foxx was enjoying his lifestyle. He had earned respect for his acting, comic, and musical abilities, and he had enough money to go out and enjoy himself. However, he was not followed everywhere he went by photographers or bothered by fans. "Where I am right now it's cool," he said. "It's just enough crazy." [59]

Things would change in a few months, however, when *Ray* was released to the public. The performance that had been so impressive on the set would also impress audiences and critics, earning Foxx national recognition and paving the way for a visit to the Oscars.

Chapter 6

Award Winner

oxx was poised to earn much more notice for his work than he ever had before. He had already earned acclaim for his dramatic acting, most recently in *Redemption* and *Collateral,* but both these performances would be dwarfed by the accolades he received when *Ray* was released in the fall of 2004.

Just a few years earlier, when he was being recognized for his role as Bundini Brown in *Ali,* Foxx had flippantly said that if he ever won an Academy Award he would wear it on a gold chain around his neck. At the time, his chances of being named Best Actor seemed remote. Now, however, winning the Oscar, and making some big career changes, seemed like a realistic possibility.

Enjoying a Hit

Foxx's hard work on the set of *Ray* paid off with a movie that even Ray Charles was proud of. Charles died in June 2004, but about a month before his death he listened to a rough cut of the film. He liked what he heard and gave the movie his approval.

Critics also gave the film a thumbs-up when it was released in October 2004. Foxx received credit for capturing the nuances of Charles's personality and the depth of his musical talent with amazing accuracy. "Jamie Foxx gets so far inside the man and his music that he and Ray Charles seem to breathe as one," wrote reviewer Peter Travers. "Foxx's fierce, funny, deeply felt performance deserves to be legendary." [60]

Foxx enjoyed the international publicity tour that came with the promotion of the movie. The tour included interviews and

Foxx's superb acting in Ray *resulted in his receiving a Best Actor Oscar nomination in 2005.*

parties, putting him in the social spotlight where he excelled. During the Toronto film festival, he spent $13,000 on champagne in one night at a Toronto nightclub. At another Toronto event he performed a swinging version of "Splish Splash," originally performed by singer Bobby Darin, with actor Kevin Spacey, who was at the festival because he had played Darin in the movie *Beyond the Sea.* Even the experienced partygoer Foxx was excited by that evening. "At first, we're just wowin' out and talkin' trash, but when Kevin steps in, it elevated the party," Foxx said. "If you could see people's faces, they were like, 'This is surreal.' Think about how classic that is! That's some history—an Oscar-winning actor onstage letting his hair down. Man!"[61]

Sad Turn of Events

That exciting evening during the Toronto Film Festival was one of many good times Foxx had that year. In 2004, the year that Foxx was establishing himself as a certified, talented star, a sad event also occurred in his life. His grandmother, Estelle Talley, died at age ninety-five. She had Alzheimer's disease, and although in her later years she had not always understood what was going on around her, Foxx believed she had understood when he would tell her about his success. "I've always known that she loves me," he said. "She smiles a little, and I know in my heart that she can feel what I'm telling her."[62]

Talley had made Foxx believe in himself and would not let him accept failure. Foxx now gave her credit for his success, noting that she gave him the self-discipline he needed as a performer. Although she had been ailing and her death was not unexpected, the loss of his grandmother left a void in Foxx's life that even his success could not fill. Foxx's grandfather had died when he was seventeen, and his relationship with his mother and father remained strained. His grandmother had been the relative he had the deepest connection with.

Oscar Contender

The work ethic his grandmother had instilled in him lived on in Foxx, and soon he began reaping its rewards. Foxx's interpretation of Charles's life was so good that he was nominated for an Oscar for Best Actor in January 2005. This was a huge accomplishment for a star who had been looked upon mainly as a comedian, not as a musician or dramatic actor. Talk of his winning intensified as the awards ceremony drew near. "It's the most unpredictable year at the Academy Awards in a long time," wrote Mike Szymanski in an Oscar preview story. "There's only one lock, and that is for Jamie Foxx, who's nominated for best actor. . . . If he doesn't walk away with a trophy, that will be the night's biggest surprise."[63]

Foxx made it no secret that he wanted an Oscar. He had been working for years to keep his career alive and set himself apart. Finally, when a role that seemed to have been tailor-made for him came his way, he had made the most of it. Now he was hoping for the payoff. He likened his drive to succeed in his career to an athlete's desire to win the big game. "If I'm playing basketball, I wanna go to the championship," he said. "If I'm playing hockey, I want the Stanley Cup."[64]

Reaping the Rewards

Just having his name mentioned in conjunction with the Oscar statue helped Foxx's career. He was featured in publications including *Rolling Stone*, *Ebony*, and *People Weekly* and made appearances on television shows such as *The Oprah Winfrey Show*, *The Tonight Show with Jay Leno*, and *The Late Show with David Letterman*. He no longer had to settle for mediocre scripts and mindless comedies. "[The Oscar buzz] helps in so many ways," Foxx said. "It means I'm walking in the right direction as far as having a career where I'll be offered parts that have meat on them. I'll be able to get up into that room where they hold the good stuff."[65]

Foxx continued to enjoy his star status, throwing celebrity-oriented parties at his California home. He shot hoops with basketball superstar Shaquille O'Neal in the backyard; threw parties for Sean Combs, rhythm and blues artist Mya, and rapper Jay-Z;

Foxx entertains the audience on **The Tonight Show with Jay Leno.**

Striking Out

Foxx loved to entertain celebrities, and the former high school sports star still enjoyed playing sports as well. He was able to combine those two interests on his backyard basketball court, called the "Foxx Hole." There he has played basketball with National Basketball Association (NBA) superstar Shaquille O'Neal as well as NBA players Paul Pierce and Bryon Russell. He also played pool with Pierce and softball with Russell, and noted that Russell was a deceptively good bowler.

Bowling was one sport Foxx admitted he had not mastered. "That's the one thing I really feel bad that I can't do, and people challenge me on that," he said in a 2004 article in *USA Today* titled "The Art and Soul of Jamie Foxx."

and watched Bobby Brown and Whitney Houston do karaoke. He commented that his agenda in life was to "inspire and do great things with great people, and have fun." He added, "If you are not having fun and people around you are not having fun, then what's it all worth?" [66]

The broad-based critical acclaim that had previously eluded him also led to some changes in the way Foxx managed his career. Around the time *Ray* was released, Foxx felt that he needed people who had experience working with award-winning stars to help him manage his career at its new level. He broke his ties with the publicist he had been working with since the beginning of his career. He hired Alan Nierob, who also managed the careers of Mel Gibson and Denzel Washington. Drawing parallels between Charles's life and his own, Foxx noted that there had been some people who worked with Charles to a certain point in his life and others who took him to the next level. Foxx was climbing to the top of the ladder and wanted to hire people who had experience with Hollywood's elite.

Accolades

The Oscar was not the only award Foxx was in contention for that year. He also received a Breakthrough Award, which honors up-and-coming performers and filmmakers, for Best Actor at the Hollywood Awards Gala Ceremony in the fall of 2004. At the Screen Actors Guild (SAG) Awards, he won the award for an Outstanding Performance by a Male Actor in a Leading Role.

Foxx's work in *Ray* also earned him the Broadcast Film Critics' Best Actor award, and at the Toronto International Film Festival he received a standing ovation for his role in the film. Although Foxx had always striven to have his ability recognized and to reach the top he was astonished by all that was happening to him. "I think this year is what we call 'beyond my wildest dream' because I never dreamed anything quite like this,"[67] Foxx said.

At the Golden Globe awards in January 2005, he was nominated for three acting awards. His work in *Redemption* earned him a nomination as Best Actor in a TV or Movie Miniseries, and he was also nominated as Best Supporting Actor in a Drama for his role as Max in *Collateral*. For his role in *Ray*, he was nominated in the Best Actor in a Motion Picture Comedy or Musical category. He received a Golden Globe award for his work in *Ray*, and the win made him the favorite to capture an Oscar.

Claiming the Statue

Foxx was nominated in two categories at the 2005 Academy Awards, as Best Supporting Actor for *Collateral* and as Best Actor for *Ray*. With those nominations he made history as the first African American to be nominated in two categories. He was pitted against well-known actors such as Clint Eastwood and Leonardo DiCaprio for the Best Actor award, but entertainment writers said that Foxx was the favorite to win. While Morgan Freeman won the award for Best Supporting Actor, Foxx proved the critics' predictions correct and won the Academy Award for Best Actor in 2005. He became the third African American to win the award, joining Sidney Poitier and Denzel Washington in that esteemed category.

In his speech at the awards ceremony, Foxx first gave credit to the man he portrayed in the movie, Ray Charles. As he had done after accepting the Golden Globe and SAG awards, he led the audience in a brief sing-along of Charles's "What'd I Say?" He then encouraged the audience to applaud Charles for his musical legacy and thanked Charles for living that legacy.

In accepting the Best Actor Oscar, Foxx gave credit to the man he portrayed, Ray Charles.

In his typical outgoing style, Foxx celebrated his victory all night and did not let the statue out of his sight. At 11 o'clock the next morning the subdued and tired actor still had it with him. An assistant took it out of a velvet bag so he could hold it while posing for one more photo. Then he got into a limousine that took him to the set of the movie he was working on.

The Big Awards

Foxx's daughter, Corrine, saw him win the Academy Award for Best Actor, but she was not as impressed as he might have expected. For her, the Oscars were just a warm-up for the real awards show. She was thinking ahead at the Oscars, and afterward she asked, "Dad, after this, can we go to the big awards?" People.com reported.

In Corrine's mind, the "big awards" were the Nickelodeon Kids' Choice Awards.

Being a loving father, Foxx complied. In April, a few months after the Oscars, he not only went to the awards but appeared on the show. He brought back memories of the movie *Ali* as he did a Rock 'Em Sock 'Em Robots skit on the show.

Foxx appears at Nickelodeon's 17th Annual Kids' Choice Awards with his daughter, Corrine.

A-Lister

Before winning the Oscar, Foxx had received some counseling from high-level Hollywood stars on how to react to the increased attention it would bring to his career. Tom Hanks, Denzel Washington, and Al Pacino all contacted him with congratulations and advice. "Just keep doin' what you're doin'," Foxx said Washington told him. "If you win or if you lose, keep walkin' in the same direction." [68] His colleagues did not want Foxx to let his increased fame go to his head. They wanted him to remain the same dedicated performer he had been, and his director in *Ray* shared those views. "I always tell him, 'Stay focused on the work,'" Hackford said. "'Don't succumb to all this amazing hoopla.'" [69]

The Oscar would have an impact on Foxx's life and career, but he had been such a favorite for the award that no huge change occurred overnight. Over the course of the past months he had been increasingly recognized for his work and rewarded for his achievements. He used his newfound status and the buzz surrounding his most recent movies to seize the top-tier roles that had not been offered to him before. He was also able to get backing for ideas that had long been in the back of his mind. He mentioned an idea for a project called *Damage Control* to director Michael Mann, who took the idea to a movie studio that made a commitment to back the project. To have someone take action on his ideas so quickly had been almost unheard-of in his career, and Foxx was amazed at his own success.

Disappointing Oscar Follow-Up

Foxx's career hit a minor snag a few months after his Oscar victory with the release of a mediocre action-adventure movie. His first film to be released after his Acadamy Award win, *Stealth* also featured Josh Lucas and Jessica Biel. Unfortunately for Foxx, the movie, about an airplane that controls itself and becomes a menace after it becomes too independent, did not succeed at the box office.

The movie had been filmed in March 2004, months before Foxx was being lauded for his roles in *Ray* and *Collateral*. Foxx had been looking for work, and he had taken a supporting role in the film for the opportunity to work with director Rob Cohen. As had often happened before, his performance was one of the few bright spots in a mediocre movie. "Jamie Foxx, who clearly signed on for this long before *Ray*, brings some mild humor to a supporting role but then disappears early on; a smart move for him, a disappointment for us,"[70] wrote reviewer Stephen Whitty.

Star Power

Just as in his earlier career, Foxx refused to let one bad movie discourage him and kept looking for better roles. He did not relax and rest on the acclaim that had come with his Oscar win. He knew what it was like to have few movie offers come his way, and now that he was in demand he took advantage of the opportunity to work with big-name stars and directors.

Before his Oscar win he had signed on to make *Jarhead,* a war movie named after the slang term for a U.S. Marine. The movie also starred Jake Gyllenhaal and was produced by Sam Mendes, a British filmmaker who had won an Academy Award for directing *American Beauty.* The movie, which was shot in late 2004 and early 2005, follows the experiences of a group of Marines during wartime, and to make the film realistic every member of the cast had to go through a boot camp experience to prepare for the film. They also had to endure the desert heat in scenes that were shot on location in Mexico.

Following *Jarhead,* Foxx was chosen to star with Colin Farrell in a movie version of the 1980s television show *Miami Vice,* which had starred Don Johnson and Philip Michael Thomas. The film was directed by Michael Mann, who had worked with Foxx in *Ali* and *Collateral.* The movie was filmed in Miami in the summer of 2005, and Foxx had the role of Detective Ricardo Tubbs, who had been played by Thomas in the TV series. The crime drama has Foxx and Farrell going after Florida drug dealers.

Making Connections

Foxx now had the Hollywood connections to make his interest in music go places, and after *Jarhead,* he polished songs on a CD

Musical Inspiration

The first single released from his *Unpredictable* CD showcased Foxx's piano background as well as rhythm and blues and rap influences. "Extravaganza," which featured a verse by Kanye West and a heavy piano track, was a mixture of rhythm and blues and rap styles. Foxx used that combination of styles on the CD in order to connect with a young audience while remaining true to his roots as a pianist. "We wanted to stay young and up," Foxx said in Austin Scaggs's article "Foxx Is 'Unpredictable'" on rollingstone.com. "But the meat of the album is more musical, more piano—back to how I really get down."

titled *Unpredictable*. The album was a mixture of styles, with songs influenced by rap music, gospel, and soul. It featured songs with Kanye West and rapper 50 Cent, and other guest performers on the album included Busta Rhymes, Pharrell Williams, Ludacris, and Twista. Most of the songs were recorded in a studio on a bus owned by rap producer Timbaland while Foxx was making *Miami Vice*. "I'd come right off the set, get on the bus and keep cutting and grinding,"[71] Foxx said.

The single "Gold Digger" with West was released in 2005 and hit No. 1 on Billboard's Hot 100 chart. Other songs on Foxx's CD included "Extravaganza," about a man who has so much fun one night that the next day he cannot remember what happened, and "Till I Met Your Sister," about a guy who goes to pick up his date, starts flirting with the girl who answers the door, and finds out she's his date's sister.

In addition to making an album with people who had powerful connections in the music industry, Foxx also prepared to make a movie with some well-known stars. In 2005 he agreed to make

After achieving success as a movie star, Jamie Foxx is determined to stay on top of his profession.

the movie *Dreamgirls,* an adaptation of a Broadway musical about a trio of black female singers who go from soul music to the pop charts. Beyoncé, Usher, and Eddie Murphy were also slated to be in the production, which would be directed by Bill Condon. Producers initially thought that Foxx's salary might be too high for their budget because of his Oscar win, but he lowered his demands once he heard that Murphy and Beyoncé were also in the movie. He admired both stars and was happy to be part of the production even if it meant less money.

Foxx is not about to rest now that he has made it to the top. He realizes that with all the attention he has won, he runs a risk of letting his ego get too big. He could easily spend too much time basking in the glory of his situation, listening to others tell him how talented he is. He knows he cannot coast on the compliments that come from his achievement. Doing that brings the risk of letting his career stagnate. Having made that mistake early in his career, when he had lost his edge on the comedy stage, he is determined to keep working hard and stay on top of his career. He acknowledges the Oscar, but at the same time tries to leave it behind and work as if it had never happened. "To me, it's about just pushing forward," he says. "Everything right now, we have in the bank. I have to go back out there and keep making great decisions."[72]

Chapter 1: From Texas to L.A.

1. Quoted in Cynthia True, "Foxx, Whole," *Texas Monthly,* November 1998, p. 88.
2. Quoted in Carrie Rickey, "For Foxx, Role Sheds a Ray of Light on Race, Determination," *Philadephia Inquirer,* October 25, 2004.
3. Quoted in Luiane Lee, "Renaissance Man Foxx Prefers Comedy," *Chicago Sun Times.* www.findarticles.com/p/articles/mi_qn41 55/is_20020104/ai-n9611009.
4. Quoted in Academy of Motion Picture Arts and Sciences, Winner Actor in a Leading Role, Speech, February 27, 2005. www.oscars.org/77academyawards/winners/01_lead_actor.h tml.
5. Quoted in Academy of Motion Picture Arts and Sciences, "Winner Actor."
6. Quoted in Steven Chean, "Music Man," *USA Weekend,* October 31, 2004. www.usaweekend.com/04_issues/041031/041031 jamie_foxx.html.
7. Quoted in William Booth, "Jamie Foxx: A Star Turns," *Washington Post,* August 6, 2004.
8. Quoted in Rickey, "For Foxx, Role Sheds a Ray of Light."
9. Quoted in Darryl Howerton, "X's and Ohhhs!," *Sport,* February 2000, p. 22.
10. Quoted in Ed Gordon, "Jamie Foxx: Behind the Scenes," CBS News, November 8, 2004. www.cbsnews.com/stories/2004/ 11/08/60II/main654348.shtml.
11. Quoted in Josh Tyrangiel, "The Art of Being a Confidence Man," *Time,* October 18, 2004, p. 76.
12. Quoted in Susan Wloszczyna, "The Art and Soul of Jamie Foxx," *USA Today,* September 28, 2004. www.usatoday.com/ life/movies/news/2004-09-28-jamie-foxx_x.htm.
13. Quoted in Lee, "Renaissance Man Foxx Prefers Comedy."

Chapter 2: A Career in Comedy

14. Quoted in Sean Smith and David Ansen, "2005 Oscar Roundtable," *Newsweek,* January 31, 2005, p. 44.
15. Quoted in Elvis Mitchell, "Jamie Foxx: Underestimated from the Start, He Always Had Something Special Up His Sleeve," *Interview,* November 2004, p. 92.
16. Quoted in Howerton, "X's and Ohhhs!," p. 22.
17. Quoted in Philip Wuntch, "Blind Ambition," *Dallas Morning News,* October 25, 2004.
18. Quoted in Josh Young, "Jamie Foxx's Oscar Hunt," *Variety,* October 4, 2004, p. S46.
19. Quoted in Mitchell, "Jamie Foxx: Underestimated from the Start," p. 92.
20. Quoted in Mitchell, "Jamie Foxx: Underestimated from the Start," p. 92.
21. Quoted in True, "Foxx, Whole," p. 88.
22. Quoted in Smith and Ansen, "2005 Oscar Roundtable," p. 44.
23. Quoted in Aldore Collier, "Jamie Foxx: The Thrills and Tears of the Ray Charles Story," *Ebony,* November 2004, p. 96.

Chapter 3: Pursuing All Options

24. Quoted in Steven Lang and Marc Ballon, "Crazy Like a Foxx," *People Weekly,* January 13, 1997, p. 81.
25. Michael Sauter, "The Great White Hype," *Entertainment Weekly,* October 4, 1996, p. 72.
26. Quoted in True, "Foxx, Whole," p. 88.
27. Quoted in True, "Foxx, Whole," p. 88.
28. Mike D'Angelo, "Booty Call," *Entertainment Weekly,* August 8, 1997, p. 82.
29. Quoted in Allison Samuels, "We are losing . . . ," *Newsweek,* March 17, 1997, p. 58.
30. Quoted in Gavin Edwards, "Sly Foxx," *Rolling Stone,* November 11, 2004, p. 73.

Chapter 4: Breaking Out

31. Quoted in Gordon, "Jamie Foxx: Behind the Scenes."

32. Quoted in Young, "Jamie Foxx's Oscar Hunt," p. S46.
33. Quoted in Richard Deitsch, "Q+A Jamie Foxx," *Sports Illustrated,* July 12, 2004, p. 28.
34. Oliver Stone, "Jamie Foxx: Mastering Any Given Part," *Time,* April 18, 2005, p. 114.
35. Quoted in Howerton, "X's and Ohhhs!," p. 22.
36. Richard Schickel, "Any Given Sunday," *Time,* December 27, 1999, p. 168.
37. Allison Samuels, "Jamie Foxx Gets in the Game," *Newsweek,* January 10, 2000, p. 60.
38. Robert Koehler, "Held Up," *Variety,* May 15, 2000, p. 26.
39. Dennis Harvey, "Bait," *Variety,* September 4, 2000, p. 23.
40. Stone, "Jamie Foxx: Mastering Any Given Part," p. 114.
41. Jess Cagle, "Jamie Foxx: Ali," *Time,* January 21, 2002, p. 126.
42. Quoted in *Texas Monthly,* "A few words with . . . Jamie Foxx," March 2002, p. 56.
43. Glenn Lovell, "Breakin' Up Is Hard to Do, but Film Goes about It All Wrong," Knight Ridder/Tribune News Service, May 17, 2004.

Chapter 5: Dream Role

44. Quoted in Clarissa Cruz, "Oscar on My Mind," *Entertainment Weekly,* October 29, 2004, p. 22.
45. Quoted in Cruz, "Oscar on My Mind," p. 22.
46. Quoted in Wuntch, "Blind Ambition."
47. Quoted in Young, "Jamie Foxx's Oscar Hunt," p. S46.
48. Quoted in Wloszczyna, "Art and Soul of Jamie Foxx."
49. Quoted in Edwards, "Sly Foxx," p. 73.
50. Quoted in Wloszczyna, "Art and Soul of Jamie Foxx."
51. Quoted in Young, "Jamie Foxx's Oscar Hunt," p. S46.
52. Quoted in Cruz, "Oscar on My Mind," p. 22.
53. Quoted in Rickey, "For Foxx, Role Sheds a Ray of Light."
54. Marc Peyser, "Snap Judgment," *Newsweek,* April 12, 2004, p. 62.
55. Steven Rea, "Foxx Steals the Show in 'Collateral,'" Knight Ridder/Tribune News Service, August 11, 2004.
56. Owen Gleiberman, "A Fare to Remember," *Entertainment Weekly,* August 13, 2004, p. 59.

57. Quoted in Tom Sinclair, "Life Imitating Art," *Entertainment Weekly,* August 12, 2005, p. 78.

58. Quoted in Cruz, "Oscar on My Mind," p. 22.

59. Quoted in Allison Samuels, "Crazy Like a Foxx," *Newsweek International,* August 30, 2004, p. 50.

Chapter 6: Award Winner

60. Peter Travers, "Unchained Heart," *Rolling Stone,* November 11, 2004, p. 114.

61. Quoted in Young, "Jamie Foxx's Oscar Hunt," p. S46.

62. Quoted in Wuntch, "Blind Ambition."

63. Mike Szymanski, "Unpredictable Year Makes Forecasting Oscars Difficult," Knight Ridder/Tribune News Service, February 6, 2005.

64. Quoted in Cruz, "Oscar on My Mind," p. 22.

65. Quoted in Clarissa Cruz, "Jamie Foxx: Ray of Hope," *Entertainment Weekly,* December 31, 2004, p. 54.

66. Quoted in Young, "Jamie Foxx's Oscar Hunt," p. S46.

67. Quoted in Collier, "Jamie Foxx: The Thrills and Tears of the Ray Charles Story," p. 96.

68. SAG Awards Official Web Site, "11th Annual SAG Awards Acceptance Speech." www.sagawards.com/11_awards_accept.htm.

69. Quoted in Jason Lynch, "Jamie Foxx: What You Need to Know," *People Weekly,* February 14, 2005, p. 79.

70. Stephen Whitty, "'Stealth' Has 'Bomb' Written All Over It," *New Jersey Star Ledger,* July 29, 2005. www.nj.com/entertainment/ledger/index.ssf?/base/entertainment-0/112261562921769540.

71. Quoted in Austin Scaggs, "Foxx Is 'Unpredictable'," Rolling Stone News, October 6, 2005. www.rollingstone.com/news/story/_id?7688061/jamiefoxx?pageid=rs.

72. Quoted in Collier, "Jamie Foxx: The Thrills and Tears of the Ray Charles Story," p. 96.

1967

Jamie Foxx is born on December 13 in Terrell, Texas.

1986

Foxx graduates from Terrell High School and attends college on a music scholarship.

1989

Foxx's interest in comedy is kindled when he goes onstage during a comedy club's open mike night.

1990

Foxx moves to Los Angeles to try for a career as a stand-up comedian.

1991

Foxx is chosen to appear on the television show *In Living Color,* remaining in the cast until the show leaves the air in 1994.

1992

A small role in the movie *Toys* is Foxx's first role on the big screen.

1995

Foxx's daughter, Corrine, is born.

1996

Foxx returns to television with his own series, *The Jamie Foxx Show.* He does voice work for the cartoon series *C-Bear and Jamal* and has small roles in the movies *The Truth About Cats and Dogs* and *The Great White Hype.*

1997

In order to keep working, Foxx takes a role in the movie *Booty Call,* which is criticized by comedian Bill Cosby for its content.

1998

Foxx is applauded for his supporting role in *The Players Club* with comedian Bernie Mac.

1999

Any Given Sunday helps Foxx break into dramatic roles in bigger movies. He also makes the comedy *Held Up.*

2000

The comedy *Bait* does little for Foxx's career.

2001

Foxx receives praise for his role as Bundini Brown in *Ali.*

2003

The poker movie *Shade* includes Foxx as part of a large cast.

2004

Foxx is lauded for his portrayal of Stan "Tookie" Williams in the television movie *Redemption: The Stan "Tookie" Williams Story.*

2005

During his breakout year, Foxx earns Academy Award nominations for his work in *Collateral* and *Ray.* He wins an Oscar for Best Actor for his role in *Ray.* Although the movie *Stealth* stalls at the box office, Foxx earns some positive comments for his acting in the movie. *Jarhead,* a movie about life in the Marines, is released.

2006

Foxx is scheduled to star with Colin Farrell in *Miami Vice* and Eddie Murphy in *Dreamgirls.*

For Further Reading

Books

Taylor Hackford, *Ray: A Tribute to the Movie, the Music and the Man*. New York: Newmarket Pictorial Moviebooks, 2004. Jamie Foxx contributes comments to this photo-heavy book that discusses the movie *Ray*.

Geoffrey M. Horn, *Jamie Foxx*. Milwaukee: Gareth Stevens, 2005. An easy-to-read biography capturing Foxx's life.

Periodicals

Aldore Collier, "Jamie Foxx: The Thrills and Tears of the Ray Charles Story," *Ebony*, November 2004.

Ronald Eniclerico, "Jamie Foxx, Actor, Comedian, and Singer," *Current Biography*, May 2005.

Elvis Mitchell, "Jamie Foxx: Underestimated from the Start, He Always Had Something Special Up His Sleeve," *Interview*, November 2004.

Web Sites

The Internet Movie Database (www.imdb.com). A search for Jamie Foxx will bring up a biography of Foxx as well as lists of his performances. Links provide more information on his movies, television shows, and other performances.

MTV (www.mtv.com). Video clips, pictures, and information on Foxx's career are available on the site's Jamie Foxx biography.

People (www.people.com). The online home page of *People* magazine provides the latest information on Foxx and other celebrities.

Works Consulted

Periodicals

William Booth, "Jamie Foxx: A Star Turns," *Washington Post*, August 6, 2004.

Jess Cagle, "Jamie Foxx: Ali," *Time*, January 21, 2002.

Clarissa Cruz, "Jamie Foxx: Ray of Hope," *Entertainment Weekly*, December 31, 2004.

————, "Oscar on My Mind," *Entertainment Weekly*, October 29, 2004.

Mike D'Angelo, "Booty Call," *Entertainment Weekly*, August 8, 1997.

Richard Deitsch, "Q+A Jamie Foxx," *Sports Illustrated*, July 12, 2004.

Tirdad Derakhshani, "Names in the News," Knight Ridder/Tribune News Service, March 1, 2005.

Gavin Edwards, "Sly Foxx," *Rolling Stone*, November 11, 2004.

Owen Gleiberman, "A Fare to Remember," *Entertainment Weekly*, August 13, 2004.

Dennis Harvey, "Bait," *Variety*, September 4, 2000.

Darryl Howerton, "X's and Ohhhs!," *Sport*, February 2000.

Robert Koehler, "Held Up," *Variety*, May 15, 2000.

Steven Lang and Marc Ballon, "Crazy Like a Foxx," *People Weekly*, January 13, 1997.

Glenn Lovell, "Breakin' Up Is Hard to Do, but Film Goes about It All Wrong," Knight Ridder/Tribune News Service, May 17, 2004.

Jason Lynch, "Jamie Foxx: What You Need to Know," *People Weekly*, February 14, 2005.

Marc Peyser, "Snap Judgment," *Newsweek*, April 12, 2004.

Steven Rea, "Foxx Steals the Show in 'Collateral,'" Knight Ridder/Tribune News Service, August 11, 2004.

Carrie Rickey, "For Foxx, Role Sheds a Ray of Light on Race, Determination," *Philadephia Inquirer,* October 25, 2004.

Allison Samuels, "Crazy Like a Foxx," *Newsweek International,* August 30, 2004.

———, "Jamie Foxx Gets in the Game," *Newsweek,* January 10, 2000.

———, "We are losing . . . ," *Newsweek,* March 17, 1997.

Michael Sauter, "The Great White Hype," *Entertainment Weekly,* October 4, 1996.

Richard Schickel, "Any Given Sunday," *Time,* December 27, 1999.

Tom Sinclair, "Life Imitating Art," *Entertainment Weekly,* August 12, 2005.

Sean Smith and David Ansen, "2005 Oscar Roundtable," *Newsweek,* January 31, 2005.

Oliver Stone, "Jamie Foxx: Mastering Any Given Part," *Time,* April 18, 2005.

Jane Summer, "Jamie Foxx Uses Video to Get Film Role," *Dallas Morning News,* December 27, 1999.

Mike Szymanski, "Unpredictable Year Makes Forecasting Oscars Difficult," Knight Ridder/Tribune News Service, February 6, 2005.

Teen People, "Star Woes: Their Most Embarrassing Moments," August 1, 2002.

Texas Monthly, "A Few Words with . . . Jamie Foxx," March 2002.

Peter Travers, "Unchained Heart," *Rolling Stone,* November 11, 2004.

Cynthia True, "Foxx, Whole," *Texas Monthly,* November 1998.

Josh Tyrangiel, "The Art of Being a Confidence Man," *Time,* October 18, 2004.

Philip Wuntch, "Blind Ambition," *Dallas Morning News,* October 25, 2004.

Josh Young, "Jamie Foxx's Oscar Hunt," *Variety,* October 4, 2004.

Internet Sources

Academy of Motion Picture Arts and Sciences, "Winner Actor in a Leading Role, Speech," February 27, 2005. www.oscars.org/77 academyawards/winners/01_lead_actor.html.

Associated Press, "Jamie Foxx Meets with Victims of Katrina," *USA Today,* September 8, 2005. www.usatoday.com/life/people/2005-09-08-foxx-katrina_x.htm.

Steven Chean, "Music Man," *USA Weekend,* October 31, 2004. www.usaweekend.com/04_issues/041031/041031jamie_foxx.html.

Dallas Music Guide, *Jamie Foxx Interview.* www.dallasmusicguide.com/interviews/jamiefoxx.htm.

Ed Gordon, "Jamie Foxx: Behind the Scenes," CBS News, November 8, 2004. www.cbsnews.com/stories/2004/11/08/60II/main654348.shtml.

Luiane Lee, "Renaissance Man Foxx Prefers Comedy," *Chicago Sun Times.* www.findarticles.com/p/articles/mi_qn4155/is_2002 0104/ai_n9611009.

NAACP News, "Jamie Foxx Named Spokesman for NAACP Relief Fund," September 12, 2005. www.naacp.org/news/2005/2005-09-12.html.

SAG Awards Official Web Site, "11th Annual SAG Awards Acceptance Speeches." www.sagawards.com/11_awards_accept.htm.

Austin Scaggs, "Foxx Is 'Unpredictable'," Rolling Stone News, October 6, 2005. www.rollingstone.com/news/story/_id?7688061/jamie foxx?pageid=rs.

Stephen Whitty, "'Stealth' Has 'Bomb' Written All Over It," *New Jersey Star Ledger,* July 29, 2005. www.nj.com/entertainment/ledger/index.ssf?/base/entertainment-0/112261562921769540.

Ben Widdicombe, et al., "Foxx-y Gentleman," *New York Daily News,* April 11, 2005. www.nydailynews.com/news/gossip/Story/2986 93p-255743c.html.

Susan Wloszczyna, "The Art and Soul of Jamie Foxx," *USA Today,* September 28, 2004. www.usatoday.com/life/movies/news/2004-09-28-jamie-foxx_x.htm.

Cover photo: Frank Micelotta/Getty Images Entertainment/
  Getty Images
AP/Wide World Photos, 23, 39, 65, 73, 75, 83, 84, 88
© Michael Brennan/CORBIS, 30
Columbia Pictures/Photofest, 45, 59
Corel Corporation, 20
© Chip East/Reuters/CORBIS, 56
Fotos International/Hulton Archive/Getty Images, 19
Fox Broadcasting/Photofest, 31, 34
© Nicola Goode/Universal Pictures/Bureau L.A. Collections/
  CORBIS, 78
© Nicola Goode/Universal Pictures/ZUMA/CORBIS, 66
Frank Micelotta/Getty Images Entertainment/Getty Images, 7
Mike Nelson/AFP/Getty Images, 32
NP/National Basketball Association/Getty Images, 16
© Fred Prouser/Reuters/CORBIS, 10, 13, 80
© Reuters/CORBIS, 50
Showtime Networks/Photofest, 62
© Sygma/CORBIS, 53
TriStar Pictures/Photofest, 41
20th Century-Fox Television/Photofest, 27
Universal/Photofest, 14, 69
Warner Brothers/Photofest, 43, 55

About the Author

Author Terri Dougherty has written biographies, nonfiction, and fiction books for children. *Jamie Foxx* is her eighth People in the News biography. She lives in Appleton, Wisconsin, with her husband, Denis, and three children, Kyle, Rachel, and Emily.